LETTERS TO DOROTHY

These stories, essays and poems are probably the last I shall write.

Exeter was published in *Accent* in December 1981 and *Sleep* was published in *Gay Times* in September 1989. *Adam, Tap and the Dragon* was intended to be a picture book, but the project was never finished. *How It Is* was published in *Gay Times* in March 1990.

LETTERS TO DOROTHY

David Rees

THIRD HOUSE (PUBLISHERS)

First published in 1990 by Third House (Publishers)
69, Regent Street, Exeter, EX 2 9 EG, England

Typeset by Rapid Communications Ltd, London WC1X 9NW
Printed by Billing & Sons Ltd, Worcester

Distributed in the United Kingdom and Western Europe by
Turnaround Distribution Co-op Ltd, 27, Horsell Road, London N5 1XL

Distributed in the United States of America by Inland Book Company,
254, Bradley Street, East Haven, Connecticut, 06512, U.S.A.
and
Bookpeople, 2929, Fifth Street, Berkeley, California, 94710, U.S.A.

Distributed in Australia by Wild & Woolley Pty Ltd,
16, Darghan Street, Glebe, New South Wales, 2007, Australia

Cover photograph : Ian David Baker

The living cannot understand that all these feelings that are so dear to them — all these thoughts which seem so important, really do not matter. No, we have ceased to meet on common ground.
— Tolstoy, *War and Peace*

Those images that yet
Fresh images beget
— Yeats, *Byzantium*

In memory of my Grandfather, James Rees

AN OPEN WAISTCOAT

For Hugh Brogan

Who can understand this century? This city in which I was born seventy-seven years ago has been at the dead centre of its tragedies, though you – were you a casual tourist, which I know you are not – wouldn't think so. Prague ignores our time, turns her back on it, pays homage to ages more gracious. She has good reason. She stagnates, quietly. Yet, at the dead centre of Europe, you would think she would control the entire continent. She never has.

This century, John, is the age of alone-ness. When, late at night, I look out of my window at the city spread beneath me and hear nothing but silence, I think everyone's abandoned us, Prague and me. I will cry out: 'Even the dogs have abandoned us!' Certainly *my* dog has abandoned me. He slunk round the corner one morning and disappeared for ever. I have nobody else, no relatives, no friends; though I talk with my neighbours about the likelihood of rain, glasnost in the Soviet Union, the shortage of bananas. And staring as I do every night across the city – two a.m., three a.m. – I see a lamp in an upper window of Hradčany Castle and think that it could be in the bedroom of the President of the Republic, who may also be one of the loneliest men on earth and another insomniac. I have no means of knowing, of course, whether he is; he may sleep easily. But in the blackest hours of the night I tell myself that he and I are the city's guardians, the unsleeping ones, and I imagine him looking across the Malá Strana and the Staré Mesto to make sure that my light is on, to check that I have not deserted my post.

I don't turn in until I hear the comforting bell of the Old Town Hall clock strike five. By then the dark in winter will

1

not live long, and in summer it is already buried : dawn is fashioning of my window a glowing square. I sleep till ten. At my age five hours are enough.

In the day I am without self-pity and I know that my solitude is a penalty of my work – our work. It was not a glamorous job, though some think it is. I retired at sixty-five, as other men do, with a pension. A generous pension. It is day now, Christmas Day in fact, and I have been strolling about the city as I do every morning if the weather is kind, which it has been this past week. The streets were crowded with people – the young, the old, families, solitaries like myself, a few tourists – all traipsing into churches to look at the nativities; and I noted, as I often have done, how well dressed Czech women are. They take pride in their appearance : the smart overcoats, the knee-length leather boots, the bright hats – red, yellow, blue, turquoise. English women in comparison are drab. Clothes for them are simply to cover their nakedness. How many churches did I see today? Twelve, thirteen? I didn't count. But I was appalled once again by how many fine Gothic buildings we spoiled two or three centuries ago by filling them with Baroque junk. The Cardinal Arch-bishop of Prague at that time must have had shares in a woodwork factory which turned out altar–pieces, baldachinos, cherubs, virgins, bishops, saints, and so on, of indescribable hideousness. How would you like your cherub/virgin/bishop/saint, he must have said to his parish priests; with orbs or clouds, rampant or couchant, weeping or jolly? Oh, you'd like a mitre with imitation jewels? All postures done very cheap ...

But I digress. The frailty of the old is getting off the point. I am not much interested in nativities, though I do like a good Gothic church, the Týn for example (even if from the outside it seems that Gaudi could have built it); I am more interested in people – the faces that I meet. Not those of the young. They are only aware of each other, except when they think they can get something worthwhile out of us. It is the old who catch my eye. A German I saw today : a face made flabby by too much of the wrong kind of food; all chins and wobbles. He looked like Chancellor

2

Erhard. His words caught my ear – he was expounding to three other elderly Germans on the subject of his job. He was the janitor, or maintenance man, of a private school. 'We have the biggest swimming bath in Dortmund,' he said. 'The filter dates from 1939 and it's still working ... it takes two hours to walk round our fields ... I have two dozen boilers to service and I don't mean domestic boilers ... I'm not bragging, but I'm good at my job ...'

I'll bet he is, I thought. And shivered. They always were good at their jobs, the Germans. This odious fat man and his mention of 1939 reminded me of my lover Felix. Felix the Jew.

I went last week to Mělník to buy some wine; Mělník – I don't think you've been there – is surrounded by vineyards. Underneath its church is an ossuary in which the skeletons of twenty thousand of the dead – victims of the Thirty Years' War – are neatly stacked. Leg bones are piled here, arm bones there, against the walls which are apsidal, so that the effect, as you enter, is as if you were on the stage of an opera house looking at an audience; and when I add that surmounting these heaps of bones are rows and rows of skulls, all grinning at you inanely, you will realise that it is very much indeed like being in an opera house. The theatre of the dead. Or the absurd. You feel impelled to speak, to be histrionic, to quote; but what? *I knew him well*? I said nothing. I thought of Felix whose bones are lying, I imagine, in some other ossuary with thousands of fellow Jews and homosexuals, liberals who protested, Seventh Day Adventists, gypsies; but that charnel-house is not open to the public : it is a deep pit in which were buried the skulls of Auschwitz.

The caretaker didn't bother to come inside with me. We Czechs may be well dressed, but we are lazy. In Communist countries you are paid whether you do your work properly or not; no one is going to fire you, and there is no such being as an unemployed man eager to step into your shoes. We suffer from terminal apathy : nothing, we think, will change for the better. I was alone down there with the skulls. Which, I asked myself, most resembled

Felix? He was very small, at twenty-eight (his age – and mine – in 1939) a waif-like boy, skin and bones even then. I picked out a very small skull – it has a bullet-hole, but it's more probable that Felix died in the gas chambers – and put it in my bag : a large, plastic bag which contained my shopping; some fresh pork, a jar of beetroot, some cucumbers. (I hadn't yet bought the wine.) That skull is now on my window-sill and it looks out with me at night, across Prague, to the lit window in Hradčany.

At twenty-eight I was tall, handsome, vigorous, well mus-cled, hairy from throat to toe, and like most men of that age I wanted to fuck and fuck and fuck. I wouldn't now recognize myself as I was : fifty years on, my body has altered out of all compass. Except for the genitals : curious – they never change though they have grown tired. Felix was the recipient of my sperm, and he loved my cock probing inside him, touching his skeleton, telling him that bones, the symbol of mortality (immortality?) were decently clad in flesh however – in his case – minimal, as much as I loved thrusting inside his carcass. For that is one of the pleasures of sex, is it not? Reassuring ourselves and our lovers that we are not yet mortal, that death is to be defied. Death, where is thy sting? Grave, thy victory? Sooner than we imagine.

I should not speak of him in purely sexual terms. His mind and his soul were as beautiful as his body. In the three years of our relationship we did not live together, but we were planning to do so; we signed the papers for leasing the top floor of an elegant eighteenth-century house in the Malá Strana the day Hitler marched into Prague. It was a ridiculous time to be signing papers about anything. But lovers cannot help being lovers; our talk was as much of our own private future – and buying carpets and saucepans and pillows and lampshades – as it was of what Hitler might do to Prague and to us. The last time we made love Hitler's motorcade was actually driving along the street below. We didn't get out of bed to look. Hours later I wrapped my big body round Felix's little body, as if that were enough to protect him from all harm; I gently stroked his skin to soothe away nightmare

4

as he slid towards sleep. His breath was the soughing of wind in pine trees. I listened to the rain outside – heavy, drenching rain soaking into the grateful earth. Or was God in tears for what had happened?

They rounded up his whole family. The door of his mother's flat was left open, swinging on one hinge. The interior was wrecked : as if a bomb had exploded. He never betrayed me, never, I imagine, mentioned me. No Gestapo vermin gnawed my door loose. I am a Slav.

Who can live with the knowledge of this century?

Oh, the crowds too on Boxing Day (as you call it), the feast of Stephen, more than on Christmas Day! In the church of St. Jakob (another Baroque grotesquery) I went to a carol service. You, I'm told, begin your carol services with *Once in Royal David's City*; we – we obviously would – with *Good King Wenceslas Looked Out*. Yonder peasant, who is he? Who are they all, those who throng the churches and the streets, the old women, the policemen, the young soldiers, the bored waiters, the stout concierges, the fervent acolytes at Mass, the tired tram drivers, the helpful curators of museums, the faceless government functionaries? How many are like us? Afterwards I strolled to the convent of St. Agnes but no fountain spews water there now, and ugly modern offices, the headquarters of the Communist Party, stand on what may have been the forest fence. There were no crowds here.

I crossed the river, and thinking I would look at Prague from Strahov, I trudged up through Hradčany (open even on Boxing Day) and tried not to see, as I walked by it, the Černin Palace. Memories of that building are still painful. That was where we met in the chaos at the end of the war, you an enthusiastic young Englishman, blond and clear-eyed, working for the British Council, seeking a permit for something or other from me, a minor official in the Foreign Ministry. I wanted you the moment I saw you. Which happened. And despite the dangers – the work you badgered me into – for three years we were lovers, in the apartment I'd intended for myself and Felix; I the seducer of your body and you the seducer of my – I was

5

going to say soul, but that sounds pretentious. Loyalties, perhaps. A discreet word. I'm not sure that I've ever forgiven you, though the money has been a blessing. Your man in Prague.

I did look up at the Černin, prompted by one of those ironic coincidences with which life so frequently jolts us. Two of the young lovers who roam our streets walked past (they don't, in winter, have anywhere to be private; forty years of 'socialism' has produced a chronic dearth of living accommodation : they are, as a result, celibate in their parents' flats when it is cold, but when it is warm they litter our parks, our river banks, our gardens, even our graveyards, with their tissues and condoms. What Eliot called 'other testimony of summer nights.') The boy had a radio which was, as always, playing a pop song : *I want your body next to mine*. The words, the music, produced in me a sharp thrill of desire; even at seventy-seven it can, I can, and a body next to mine would be ... oh, yes ... I thought of your body next to mine, the night of the Prague coup. February 1948. Did we ignore, as we lay in bed, Gottwald and his stinking chums parading in the street below, as Felix and I ignored Hitler nine years previously? I don't think there was any parade. No full-frontal entry. The Communist rape was a silent insertion into a dark passage.

You had to flee to England while there was still time. I haven't seen you since. So I glanced, not at the window in the Černin behind which my desk stood, the spot where we met, but at the window on another floor from which they threw my boss, Jan Masaryk. That's what they did, in effect, to us, to our relationship. Threw it out of the window. Another defenestration of Prague.

Who can survive this century?

Strahov was peaceful, as it always is : *it* survives; the good taste of its church, the cloistral calm, the thousands of dusty tomes in its library, the view of the city through the trees. It is of course as fragile as anything else. An air-raid, or neglect, could destroy it. One cannot say it has endured because people have decided it should

6

endure – it is there by sheer chance. As you are. As I am.

Sheer chance allowed us to survive the war. Which was worse – you in a London smashed by German bombs, I in a Prague jack-booted by German soldiers? Again, a sexual image comes to mind : we were made to suck their cocks. You, though tattered and torn, were not so abused. I, to escape death, literally had to suck their cocks. 'On your knees!' this stormtrooper yelled, proudly displaying a massive erection. 'Suck!' I had to repeat the procedure with dozens of others. Dozens. 'Think yourself fortunate, you Czech queer,' I was told on one occasion, 'that you aren't where most bastards of your kind have been put.' (This from a man who'd just ejaculated down my throat.) I didn't know what he meant, and I'd forgotten his remark by the time of the liberation. But I found out, as we have all found out : the pink triangle, the death camps; and I cried for my sweet, loving, dead Felix – and hoped he'd been made to wear the six-pointed star. What horrors, though, would he have suffered if he'd been ordered to wear that *and* the pink triangle?

I was fifty-seven when we were assaulted again, this time by the Russians – a rape from the east instead of the west. How vulnerable we are, landlocked and stranded in the middle of Europe! 'This dagger,' Brezhnev said, 'pointing at the heart of the Soviet Union.' Anything less like a dagger would be difficult to conceive. And Chamberlain's 'far-off country about which we know very little.' Was your peace-in-our-time merchant not aware that the distance from London to Prague is the same as the distance from London to John o' Groats?

My job, of course, made it impossible for me to have a lover; it was for our sexual preferences that your organization recruited us, so I became a single man. Did you? You'll tell me, I'm sure. The authorities here have never had the slightest suspicion! Not during the terror of Gottwald and his thugs, the grim greyness of Zapotocký, Novotný's corruptions, Husák's long boredom. In Dubček's spring I had to be careful; I could have relaxed and given myself away. In 1968 I was having sex twice a week with a prostitute who picked me up in the bar of the Hotel Europa –it's always been a good place for men. It still is. He was German, a husky, hunky lad in his twenties, a student cook from Karl-Marx-Stadt in the G.D.R. (Ridiculous name, Karl-Marx-Stadt! Imagine Prague renamed. What would it be? Gottwaldov? Husákhrad?) He reminded me of S.S. men – blue eyes, blond hair, muscles. *He* approached *me*. I brought him to my flat; he wanted me on my knees, just as those Germans did during the war. (Was one of them his father?) I refused : not *that* humiliation again, though I'd have done it with a good-looking man from any other country in the world. I said I was going to screw him, which *he* refused. He wasn't queer, he said; he had a pregnant girlfriend at home in Karl-Marx-Stadt – he simply needed money. I think he was telling the truth. I offered him twice the price he'd wanted (he was clearly an amateur; he'd requested half the going rate) and eventually he agreed. It was obvious he didn't like it at all, and that turned me on. I'd never previously considered sex as a political weapon, but that was what it was; with every thrust into this well-built Aryan he-man I thought, 'Fuck the Germans! Fuck them! *Fuck them*! FUCK THEM!'

When it was over he said it had been like a red-hot poker up his arse, and he looked as if he could kill me. I gave him the money and said, why not return for another session on Tuesday? I didn't think he would, but the desire for money, I suppose, was stronger than the pain and humiliation I'd inflicted; he arrived at exactly the appointed hour. And so it went on for six months, both of us gradually forgetting such concepts as pain and humiliation; he was beginning to enjoy it. What did he do, I asked, with the cash he earned from me? It was, if he'd saved it all, quite a considerable amount. It had mostly gone, he said, to the girlfriend in Karl-Marx-Stadt who was now the mother of his little boy. (Yet another blue-eyed Aryan, I imagine, who would today be – what – twenty-one! Yes!)

We often talked about politics. He was as anti-Russian as any Czech; he saw Dubček as a hero, a saviour. A saint. He had a photo of Dubček, he told me, on the wall of the room in which he lodged. That summer the crisis worsened; would the Russians allow Prague spring to continue : could this unlikely experiment in 'Communism with a human face' survive? No need here to repeat what happened; the world knows it only too well. Sasha Dubček, perhaps, had too human a face. Was naive. The invasion, though feared, was a terrible shock; the first I knew of it was Russian tanks rumbling beneath my windows. On that August afternoon Jurgen came at the usual hour; he had with him a banner he had painted : 'At least Hitler was polite – he declared war before he marched in.' Not quite true, I said gently. If I could have been amused in that situation I'd have laughed – this young German had become as fierce a Czech as I was when Felix vanished. I think I smiled. What was he going to do with it? 'I shall wave it at the tanks!' he declared, blue eyes blazing. But, I said even more gently, Ivan on the tank wouldn't understand it – the slogan was in Czech, and the alphabet of the average Russian soldier was Cyrillic.

It was on that occasion, while shouts, screams, bangs, the rattle of bullets, the thud of explosions, shook the street below, we ceased to be prostitute and client; we became lovers : kissing, stroking, murmuring endearments, finding each other with fingertips and tongues, eyes and skin, words and more words, as Felix and I did, as we did, John; as all lovers do, particularly when death threatens. We didn't pause to look out of the window though he wanted to. 'There'll be time for that,' I said. 'Believe me, there'll be time for that!' And in the days that followed there was. We joined the crowds, he with all the folly and fury and absurdity of youth, I with more discretion. I hurled at the occupying soldiers branches ripped from trees, garbage from dustbins, furniture, cobbles from the road; he daubed swastikas on their trucks, threw Molotov cocktails, climbed onto a tank and stuffed his shirt, petrol-soaked, down the turret : he managed to set it alight, and rolled himself clear before it exploded. But a Russian on the tank behind was coolly observing, cruelly observing; and as soon as he had the chance he fired. Another corpse:

9

slack limbs, hole in the head, bloodied mouth. Only an hour before those limbs had shuddered with life as his seed flooded my mouth.

Who can stand this century?

Why do I put all this on paper when you know it in part and you'll hear the rest next week? The urge to record so that evil will not be forgotten. I sometimes work now as a guide; I've had to take tourists to Lidice. You know the story, but you haven't been there : the village the Nazis obliterated in revenge for the murder of Heydrich. Every man was shot; every woman and child deported to concentration camps, though not one of those people had the remotest connections with Heydrich's assassins. The Germans then destroyed the village; what they could not burn or bury they removed. There is no trace of it. You see nothing at Lidice but green fields, though you experience a curiously unnatural silence. Even the birds shun it. Nearby is a museum which contains the small handful of relics that were found, and a film the Nazis themselves made of the crimes they were committing – the shooting of the men, the rounding up of the women and the children, the burning of the village.

When I was last there I was with a group of British tourists. We were unable to see the film as the projector had broken. Those comfortable, middle-class, British women, scions of your Thatcherite bourgeoisie, all said, 'I'm glad we didn't see that film. It would have been too much.' Such sentiments infuriate me, for that is how the world's atrocities are forgotten : complacent, affluent, oh, probably well-meaning people don't want their little certainties disturbed. They *should* have seen that film; they *should* have been reminded. For without reminders it is all too easy for the criminals to strike again. The same process of forgetting – the same paralysis of the imagination which is a prelude to the loss of fellow-feeling – occurs when somebody says, 'I don't want to think about AIDS ... or Stalin, or Vietnam ... I don't want to listen to Janáček or Martinu ... I don't want to know what gay men do in

10

bed.' Such people are the most dangerous on earth, and in Czechoslovakia we have had some good examples of the species. Didn't Kundera call Dr. Husák the President of Forgetting? Didn't Max Frisch point out that Dr. Beneš let in the fire-raisers? Loss of memory is the first sign of the disintegration of the personality. Yonder peasant, who is he?

But I am beginning to deliver a sermon, so I shall stop. Chekhov said in a letter to Alexander Lazarev-Gruzinsky, 'You must describe your women in such a way that the reader feels your tie is off and your waistcoat open. Women and nature both. Let yourself go.' That is what I am trying to do.

The loneliness of the lonely is never more obvious than at Christmas. People travel from each end of this country, as they do in any country, to be with their loved ones on Christmas Eve, and though they may pay lip-service in their prayers to the halt, the sick, the wretched, the alone 'and those who know not the Lord Jesus,' they soon forget them – the Felixes, the Jurgens, the you and me – in the family gatherings over carp and white wine. So it is with the greatest pleasure that I anticipate your visit. I have not seen you for forty-one years. I don't suppose, at this date, that we shall be tearing off each other's pants to grip and claw and suck and thrust, but I shall kiss you tenderly. There is much to talk about. Our jobs, for example; 'I have done the state some service.' We both have. Britain would have suffered a little without us, and I did warn you about Kim Philby – in good time too. Prague, geographically and architecturally, is a great place for spies, and I doubt that those men and women I betrayed suffered the tortures at your hands that some of our friends suffered from the K.G.B. They wouldn't have been, as I'm told Penkovsky was, placed alive in their coffins then slowly fed into the ovens of crematoria 'pour encourager les autres.' Nobody I slept with I betrayed to your secret service, to anyone's secret service. I couldn't do that. It would have been as if it was I who had shot Jurgen, who shoved

11

Felix into the gas chamber, who threw you-and-me out of the window.

I've always been grateful for the escape route, the safe houses you've provided for me, and it is a miracle that I have never had to use them. A miracle!

But who can forgive this century?

LETTERS TO DOROTHY

For Colin Bell(e)

Bratislava
May 18th.

Dear Dorothy,

I've always wanted to write to you from Bratislava; it sounds so … *esoteric*. In fact it's a most frightful dump, the only place I've been to with a motorway so close to the old city centre that the cathedral's falling down. *Dreadful* shame, as it's *terribly* ancient and had nine Hungarian *queens* crowned in it. (Thought you'd enjoy that titbit of information being a Hungarian queen yourself.) Your letter awaited us at our hotel, for which many thanks – I was interested to hear about Julian's veruccas and Sandy's warts. Really, I can't *imagine* what goes on in that relationship! Does Julian put his feet … ? Sorry to be so *clinical*. Tell Sandy there's a hospital in the Holloway Road with a laser beam that will *scorch* them off; a bit like having sand-blasting apparatus up your bum, I guess. Enough on that … I won't tire you to death with details of Prague as you know it so well. Sufficient to say it was as beautiful as ever, particularly in the hot May sun. We trolled around the Staré Mesto and stared at all the nice young men promenading up Wenceslas Street, had coffee and *divine* cake for twelve and a half pence, and I *nearly* had an encounter with a real live Czech (slim, Slavic and succulent) near the Powder Tower; yes, *really*! *He* looked and *I* looked and *he* looked again, so *I* crossed the street then came back when he didn't follow and at *last* we got talking and discovered we both *were*, and that he would like to, but *where*? Well, there wasn't a

13

convenient where and I'm too old for this kind of thing anyway, so we didn't. Jonathan meanwhile, having said I could eye up all the Czechs *and* all the Slovaks so long as he could eye up all the marauding Magyars when we get to Hungary, propped himself against a lamp-post while this contretemps was contretemping, *very* ostentatiously I thought, and pretended to read Rude Pravo, but he was holding it *upside down*. Czech is an impossible language to read anyway; doesn't seen to have any *vowels* ...

After that we *swished* over the Charles Bridge into the Lesser Town and peeped into *masses* of *delicious* Baroque churches, went up to Hradčany and St Vitus's Cathedral (simply *everybody* is buried in there including Good King Wenceslas, but no Communists of course; I wonder where they are? Did you know President Gottwald was poisoned by someone at Stalin's funeral? Came home and dropped dead.) Our hotel was good, though the English on the menu was weird, and I mean *weird* ... For breakfast we could have had (but didn't) 'Boiled eggs in glass – three pieces' and for dinner, 'Bruised foot.' Braised I suppose it was meant to be, but foot of *what*? I *dread* to *think*. Have kept the menu and will send it to Esther Rantzen.

Came to Bratislava by coach, motorway toute la route, *huge* traffic jams as we left Prague. But once we got into the countryside we knew we weren't on a Western main road – scarcely a car or a lorry for *miles*. Nice change from the M 25 at Leatherhead. Countryside pretty but most odd : all green, certainly, but such a *peculiar* green, quite unnatural; Jonathan said they've over-used their fertilisers. He's probably right; he *knows* about such things. There wasn't a single wild flower or a bird or a butterfly *anywhere*, sort of Orwellian.

Most of the other people on our tour are our age and quite interesting, with mid-European connections – there's a German Jewish lady whose entire family died in the holocaust; a Czech couple who fled to England in 1948; and some are Hungarian emigrés who are going to see relatives in Budapest. Also six young American heteros who are a *pain* : completely ignorant about Europe and so *patronising*; Reagan worshippers of course. They did *everything* quite

14

shamelessly at the back of the coach except actually *screw*; wonder what they'd say if I shoved my hand up Jonathan's shorts and *wanked* him off for all to see. And there are two English persons obviously friends of Dot's – an elderly clone with a thick bushy moustache (actually not bad-looking) whom Jonathan's christened Burt – with a *u* – who has this *very* young thing in tow, pretty boy, all sultry; looks as if he's just been fished out of the Bell – Oxfam clothes and pink hair and various parts of his anatomy *impaled* with curious lumps of *metal*. I've christened him *Agnes*. They don't seem to be getting on at *all* well – grunt in monosyllables and look at everything except each other; there's more than a *nuance*, I'd say a positive atmosphere. One of them I'm sure is going to get off with somebody else before this trip is over just to *annoy*; I'm taking bets on Burt, but Jonathan's backing Agnes. Neither of us, I can assure you, is going to be the sacrificial victim. I think it will happen in Budapest but Jonathan says they'll wait till Moscow; will report to you all the details when and as.

Stunning view from Bratislava Castle of quite the most *dreary* concrete maze of Communist Monumental workers' flats I've ever seen – castle very restored but interesting despite portraits of President Husák; time the aged fool was given the boot. What's left of the old town is nice, but dead – like a damp Sunday afternoon in Perivale. Julian, years ago, said Bratislava had the busiest cottages in Europe, but not a soul in the ones I peeped into; somebody ought to write to Čedok and complain. Cold and drizzling here and it was so *hot* in Prague! We both arrived in *shorts*! Ate a very good meal last night in an ethnic restaurant with live Slovak music, sounded sort of Hungarian, maybe because Slovaks have *cymbaloms* in their bands. *Lovely* instrument! Jonathan says it's only a de-tuned piano played with muffled drumsticks, but I think it's ever so *camp*. They ought to install one at Heaven. Went to bed early and Jonathan insisted on screwing me into the stratosphere; said we hadn't done it for *centuries*. Woke up with a headache and feeling depressed. Had a great need of peace and quiet and did not want to talk or listen to *anybody*, least of all to Jonathan's biopsy on last night's fuck – was it eight or nine on the Richter scale? – so took myself into the nearest Baroque church (a bit like Brompton Oratory in drag) and heard *Mass*. My *dear*! Can you *imagine*? I haven't been to Mass since 1972. It was all in Slovak of course so I didn't understand a *thing*. But I felt better afterwards. Isn't that *strange*?

Must cease. We depart in five minutes to catch a hydrofoil which *whirls* us down the Danube into Hungary; next stop Budapest. Am looking forward to it!

Love and kisses from –

– The Winter Queen of Bohemia XXX

Budapest
May 24th

Dear Dorothy,

Another letter! How *kind* you are! Enjoyed the gossip about Leslie's party (did Mike *really* go as the Dowager Empress of China? Where on earth did she get hold of the *fingernails*?) Wish I'd been there, would *love* to have seen that *scrumptious* Peter Smith swinging on a chandelier, and *stark* naked too! Is it as *huge* as I've been told? (I don't mean the chandelier.) You left that detail out, flower, and I *must* know. By return, please. Sorry to hear the laser is only for pregnant women (we gays lose out *all* the time), but tell Sandy freezing is quite effective and doesn't hurt a *bit*. You didn't mention Julian's veruccas …

Well … Burt and Agnes nearly came to blows on the hydrofoil, and, if they had, Jonathan and I would *both* have lost our bets. It was Agnes's fault (dizzy queen); she let herself get chatted up almost all the way into Hungary by this *enormous* Viking from Reykjavik, a bearded blond in shorts with hairy muscly thighs that went up and up and *up* like tree trunks, rape and pillage just *oozing* out of his ice-blue eyes … *wonderful*! Twenty years ago I'd have had my legs in the air at the *bat* of one of those sexy eye-lids … Anyway, Burt pretended to look at a magazine and stared out of the window and smoked cigarettes and drank *oodles* of slivovitz as if nothing in the world was wrong, but he didn't deceive *me*. *No*! When Agnes eventually came tripping

16

back, all smiles for the first time in a week, Burt threw his slivovitz into her face. 'D-ra-*ma*!' I hissed in Jonathan's ear, but he's such an old fuddy-duddy these days he didn't even glance up, just went on reading his book, *Disused Rituals of the Serbian Orthodox Church*. But it was all a big let-down in the end; Agnes meekly wiped off the slivovitz with a tissue, said nothing, and sat beside Burt, arms folded and an expression of injured innocence on her ugly mug. And so we reached Budapest ...

Enjoyed the hydrofoil, particularly going round the Danube Bend, sort of like the Rhine gorge – Wagnerian with forests and a monastery on the cliffs at Estergom, all rather beautiful; you could imagine loreleis *luring* men to certain *doom*. And the hydrofoil was a splendid way to have first impressions of Buda and Pest which look *at* their river, not like London ignoring the Thames as if it's a bad smell; first sight of the Parliament Building quite stunning, a real fairy-tale palace, Austro-Hungarian imperial and nineteenth-century. Our hotel is in downtown Pest, de luxe with *marvellous* food. Hungary very westernised compared with Czechoslovakia, Coca-Cola signs and goodies galore in the shops, traffic impossible, so much of it you can't cross the Rákóczy Út any hour of the day or night for fear of being *hewn* to pieces. The smog is like Los Angeles. Weather sunny, humid, warm. Traipsed around the city on foot (Jonathan refused to take the metro for some reason) and got absolutely *frazzled* doing all the tourist things – art gallery (something by everybody including Constable – most peculiar to find a picture of Hampstead Heath in *Hungary*, and, equally odd, snow-bound landscapes by Gauguin of all people), Matthias church (sightseers packed in like *sardines*), old Buda which is *very* pretty, the Turkish bath (actually built by the Turks in sixteen something or other, still has a gold crescent on its dome and must be the world's oldest functioning bath-house. We couldn't find a door to get into it, though we could hear men's voices on the other side of the wall; the thought of magnificent, moustachioed, marauding Magyars, *hordes* of Huns hurtling over the hills on horse-back, and now prancing around *naked* in the steam, drove Jonathan

17

nearly *frantic*. And who paid for that later? *Me*, of course. Jonathan went on for *ages* about bums (one of his favourite topics but not one of mine), then *threw* me onto the hotel bed for another quick excursion into the stratosphere. The walls are *desperately* thin and you could have heard his orgasm – he pants like a pair of bellows – in *Oslo*. Whatever Burt and Agnes thought I cannot *imagine* – they're in the next room, number thirty (Dirty Burty from Number Thirty) – or the two home-counties ladies on the other side, very twin-set and pearls and Maggie Thatcher hair-dos; 'Aren't the streets of this city so *depressing*?' they fluted, and gave me a sour look when I said I've seen worse in London which, unlike here, has mugging *and* glue-sniffing *and* graffiti *and* dog-shit. I hope Jonathan will soon stop wanting to fuck like Genghis Khan – he's *menopausal*, poor thing – and return to his usual self. It gave me another headache and I felt sort of defiled, which I know is daft as we've been lovers for a quarter of a century. So I went off on my own, this time to a synagogue. A service had just begun, but they let me in; I suppose, ha-ha, they thought I was a *man*! I had to wear a skull-cap : there was a box of paper ones at the door – rather fetching – like hats from Christmas crackers. They dish them out to anyone bareheaded, but make you return them to the box when you leave. *Weird*.) Sorry about this long parenthesis, ought to be in the Guinness Book of Records. Where was I? Yes, tourist things. I think I need a vodka tonic and a new paragraph ...

... The crown jewels of St. Stephen. *Very* impressive, dating from nine hundred and something and looking brand new, but must, like the bath-house, be the oldest in the world. Nice coffee-shops, better even than those in Prague, better coffee at any rate. A great many houses here are pockmarked with bullet-holes, from 1956 I guess, or 1944. Our guide is *awful*, unlike the Czech guide who couldn't do enough for us. This one pointed at a statue near the Parliament Building (we were doing a quick coach trip round the city) and said it was Béla Bartók, but it wasn't. I went back next day to have a look; Bartók is one of my *heroes*. It was somebody else. So I simply told *everyone* on our tour and they were *frightfully* cross anyway

18

as our guide does *fuck* all, and they said they wouldn't give him a tip when we leave. Not for nothing am I known as a shit-stirrer ...

D-ra-*ma*! Jonathan went to bed last night before I did; I stayed downstairs drinking tokay with the home-counties ladies (they certainly knock the old vino back). When I went up to our room J. was watching the English-language programme on TV, and he said, 'The government's fallen.' I said, hopefully, 'Maggie?' and *he* said, 'No, you fool. The *Hungarian* government.' Yes! After thirty-two years old Kadar's on his bike. History is being made under our very *noses*! Next morning I *dashed* down to the foyer and it was full of Russian troops!!! I thought, *eek*!, and sidled out into the Rákóczy Út, expecting tanks and barricades. No such luck. Everything super-normal; traffic jams, petrol fumes, and crowds of Budapestis hurrying to work. Maybe a few more people than usual buying newspapers. Boring! The Russian soldiers turned out to be a regiment of Mongolians (many of them very cute; I like those slanting eyes) here for their annual holidays. So *no* drama, alas. Life can be such a bitch.

      Love and kisses from –
      – Maria Theresa, Empress of Austria-Hungary XXX

                Szentendre
                May 30th

Dear Dorothy,

I must say I did like Budapest. A big, bustling capital that makes Prague look a mite *provincial*. (Though Prague is still my number one most beautiful city in Europe.) Really lots to do and see; attractive buildings, wide tree-lined boulevards, street life, shops, parks. A bit like Paris with cymbaloms. Now we're somewhere absolutely *different*, a village in the country with Hungarian peasant life albeit somewhat touristified. Jonathan was in *raptures* when we discovered a Serbian Orthodox church, complete with domes like *onions* or maybe even *bunions*. Can't think what it's doing *here* such a long way from Serbia, wherever Serbia may be which I'm not too sure of anyway. It's ever so pretty inside with ikons all over the place, but I was disappointed it's not used now; I was hoping for *wonderful* ceremonies with archimandrites and patriarchs parading up and down simply *everywhere* in those super hats like inverted saucepans, incense thick as pea-soup fog, Orthodox choirs, smells and bells *galore*, something to make the Anglicans look like Quakers or Shakers, but no! It's really hot here, eighty-seven or eighty-eight, so we eat out in garden restaurants or in pavement cafés and watch the boys go by. It's a good year for *legs* I've decided, a lot of them about. All bronzed and hairy in tight short shorts which makes Jonathan drone on about *bums*. Pleasant just strolling around; tree-shaded village square called Karl Marx Ter, which is a bit stupid as the newest house in it was built three hundred years before the old boy began the first sentence of *Das Kapital*; little cobbled alleys; glimpses of the Danube; and old women in black, bent double under *sacks* of *cabbages*, shooing chickens out of the way.

No letter from you but wasn't expecting one; you probably thought Szentendre, where's that? Never heard of it, mail can't possibly be delivered *there*, but I hope to find in Moscow a *massive* missive. Main news is I won my bet!!! Big explosion *did* occur in Budapest and Burt *was* the instigator. *Well* ... Jonathan and I were lying on our beds at the hotel, reading. (He's now deep into *Ikons of Russia*, the same book Raisa gave horrid Nancy, do you remember? And Nancy went all miffed about it when Raisa presented another copy of the same book to a minor flunky at the American Embassy.) I was reading Patricia Nell Warren; I *do* like her (though my theory is she's a he, knows *far* too much about what *we* get up to.) *Anyway* ... I *suppose* I must have been aware of the creak of bed-springs in the next room but wasn't really listening till I heard the door open and slam shut, *then* the most almighty row with Agnes screaming her tits off, and *things* being thrown all round the place; one object smashed into the wall so hard the photo of the beach at Yalta on *our* wall went quite *crooked*: so I got off the bed and opened the door a *crack* just to see who would come out of number thirty – I mean there just

20

had to be a man in there who wasn't Agnes or Burt, and I wasn't wrong. *No!* It was one of the hotel waiters, and Agnes must have caught Burt in flagrante delict*u* (I do so prefer the fourth declension to the third; delict*o* sounds so *common*). I hadn't the heart to tell Jonathan it was the same waiter he'd been fantasising about at breakfast, a butch rough-trade number with Imre Nagy moustaches and – I imagine – hairy as a werewolf; J. was saying over the yoghurt and cornflakes that he could just see this *Magyar* like in one of those Jancso films stampeding across the steppes on a stallion, looking for a decent bit of *pillage*, but I said he was *utterly* unattractive (which he is) even though the bulge in his about-to-split trousers in hee-*uge*. (Hee-*uge* is my new word. Do tell Ian and Mark.) *And the consequence was* ... Agnes has vanished. Maybe she's defected, asked for political asylum or something, though I guess the Hungarian authorities are in too much of a tizzy over their new government to be bothered with a limp Brit queen complaining about sexual har*ass*ment. I hope she's gone off with the waiter. In fact I think she probably *has* gone off with the waiter. (Neither of them were to be seen at dinner.) They're *magnificently* suited.

After this Jonathan got very amorous (well, what went on in number thirty gave even *me* a teensy twinge in the gonads) and very gentle, so we made love *properly* (I mean it wasn't I-hear-volcanoes-waterfalls-symphonies stuff, nor the in-two-three, up-two-three, down-two-three, dazzle-us-all-with-your-terrific-technique-darling-two-three bit) but ... ever so *nice*. I really enjoyed it for once, and I do love Jonathan, even though that isn't always obvious; I honestly don't know how I could *live* if he left me, which he isn't going to do in a *century* of Sundays, thank Christ.

Nothing to do here in the evenings which is a welcome change after relentless sightseeing and concerts and operas in Prague and Budapest. (Did I tell you we saw *La Bohème* in Budapest? In *Hungarian*, my dear; can you imagine? I loved it of course, and *soaked* several Kleenexes. And we heard Bartók's Concerto for Orchestra at the Vigadó Hall; it needs *two* harps. I always think *two* harps inspiring, don't you?) We sit out these warm evenings in the street cafés and get gently squiffy on Hungarian plonk (very good and it doesn't produce gut corrosion like Spanish Château El Harpic). Discussing ballet last night with the two home-counties ladies (both dress in *hideous* matching suits of deepest Tory *blue*) and said I was looking forward to the *Bol*shoi in Moscow; they said, 'Oh! The Bol*shoi*' – tones of revulsion as if they'd seen a dead rat – and they went on about how inferior Russian ballet is to the heydays of Dame Ninette and Dame Margot; honestly they're so fucking chauvinist they think paradise on earth is East Finchley or *Penge*. They haven't enjoyed *anything* on this trip – just looked for whatever might confirm their pre-judged opinions – can't *think* why they came to Eastern Europe in the first place. So I said a few outré things on the subject of Nureyev which shut them up, then I *floated* off down the street, *waving* my handbag as only a real queen can, Jonathan in tow. He said I was a *frightful* embarrassment, which surprised me no end. *I* don't think I'm an embarrassment, do you?

Tomorrow we return to Budapest for the flight to Moscow. *Moscow, Moscow*! – as the three sisters said to Chekhov. Goodnight, princess.

Kisses from –
– Zsa-Zsa Gabor XXX

Moscow
June 4th

Dear Dottie-Dot,

So they've *both* got veruccas now! *And* warts! How on *earth* do they manage it? *Do* give them my condolences, and tell them I've bought them a little prezzy, a souvenir of Holy Mother Russia. So *The Stud* is sold, is it! And *The Mare on Heat*'s gone bankrupt, *The Nag's Head* is empty these days, and every queen in town's on view at *The Colt*! Well … Plus ça change. What a fickle lot we are! It's just two months since *The Mare on Heat* went women only on alternate fifth Saturdays, *The Stud* was packed to the eyebrows, *The Nag's Head* had a face-lift and a cabaret of abseiling lesbians in leather, and nobody, simply nobody who is *anybody*, would be seen *dead* at *The Colt*! That's gay life for you …

Well … Moscow is quite something. A much more *normal* city than I'd anticipated, with rush hours and traffic jams just like London. Pavement cafés full of glasnosting Russians, all very friendly and speaking *marvellous* English; *vast* quantities of gorgeous Impressionists at the Pushkin; and a *super* metro, not a bit like the Northern Line at Collier's Wood, with the *campest* chandeliers you could imagine. (I'd love to see Peter Smith swinging on one of these; whatever would Raisa and Mikhail say? And it really is *that* big? You're exaggerating again, dear; not that I'm a size queen. *No*! Never was.) Lots of perestroika; we were stuck in one of their *hee*-uge traffic jams and I was staring out of the coach window into an office – filing cabinets and boring-looking clerks in suits, *ever* so dull I thought, rather like the Dalston branch of the Abbey National – and our guide said to me, 'That's the headquarters of the K.G.B.' 'The *K.G.B.*!' I shrieked. I mean, I wouldn't know where M.I.5 *is*, would you? And I daresay if we asked, some London cop would fling us into a paddy waggon. Glasnost too in the Kremlin. 'That's the Praesidium of the Supreme Soviet,' our guide said, pointing at the ugliest building in Russia, about two yards away … well, you can't get into Downing Street *at all*, let alone within two yards of Number Ten. The dimbo Yanks on our tour I told you about are getting dimber than ever. 'Can we go in there?' one of them said to our guide. 'What for?' she asked, and he said, 'I wanna rap with Gorby.' *Well* … what *can* one say? We just laughed, but the guide looked blanker than blank. 'What is rap?' she wanted to know.

The Yanks then decided to join the queue in Red Square and see Lenin. This way to the tomb … Last thing I wanted, and I said so to Jonathan. He agreed. I mean, standing in line for an hour and three quarters just to squint at some pocky old *corpse* … Bit like in those Italian basilicas with saints' bones all over the place; in Padua I remember people queuing up in a side-chapel to touch a reliquary with a bit of St. Anthony in it : when I looked to see what actual bit of him it was it turned out to be the sacred *foreskin*! All shrivelled up and horrible and leathery; I'd rather get my hands round Peter Smith's *any* day of the week. (Does he *have* one? Forgot to ask.) *Well* ... these Yanks were wearing shorts; I told them they wouldn't get *near* Lenin dressed like that – it would be like attempting to go inside a Catholic church in Spain wearing a sleeveless, see-through vest. They just sniggered in a superior fashion, imagining no doubt their American accents would be a passport to anything including Lenin, but I wasn't wrong. *No!* They weren't even allowed to join the queue! And serve them right, I say.

Red Square is nice, very *big*, and I was *completely* out of my box last night in one of its bars on a bottle of *excellent* Stolichnaya in the company of guess who? *Agnes!* Burt's been pouring out his troubles to Jonathan (*men's* talk) so I took Agnes under my wing for *girls'* talk. *Anyway* ... she *did* go off with the waiter (who's called Istvan and he's as hairy as a *yeti* – all over including down his back. Ugh!) Bliss it was, he said, particularly as Burt is apparently quite hopeless in the sack; I said did Istvan use a condom, and Agnes, very self-satisfied, said, 'A condom? He filled at least two *dozen!*' I said to Jonathan later her arse must now be as squashy as a second-hand marshmallow, and he said I was absolutely *disgusting*, which surprised me no end. *I* don't think I'm disgusting, do you? *Well* ... Burt and Agnes are back together again in a sort of sulky truce. I said to Jonathan, I don't want to sound all smug and hoity-toity and holier than thou, but it didn't seem to *me* to be *any* kind of way to run a relationship. He agreed.

What else? The GUM Store is *frightful*; in fact all the shops very drab after Budapest and Prague, *immense* queues and the only veggies to be had are *cucumbers*. But hotel very good, and we met two gay Russians at the bar one night; they said AIDS was much more *rampant* here than the government says it is, and gay life is furtive and fumbling and infrequent, and did we have condoms to sell as they think their Communist brands are below par. (K.G.B. sticks pins in them or something?) I said Jonathan and I, though we still enjoy looking and having our fantasies, stopped *tearing* other men's knickers off *years* ago (I mean,

24

at our age!) and therefore we didn't see much point in investing our hard-earned pennies in condoms. It's no bad thing these days, I said to myself, to be an elderly, raddled queen like me. (Or *you*.) Our bed-hopping days were *well* before AIDS, and even if we watched the nineteen seventies with a kind of green envy (too old to join in) it was probably a bonus in the long run being born *decades* before the Act. How *ghastly* it would be at twenty-two to find you had AIDS ...

Went to *Aida* at the *Bol*shoi. It was in Russian, a great improvement on Italian I thought. *Not* my favourite opera (though I *worship* Act Two and all those *processions*.) Russian made the priests and priestesses sound like an Orthodox choir. *Super*! If the great Giuseppe could have heard it he'd have swopped languages *instantly*. St. Basil's is something out of Disneyland, but the cathedrals in the Kremlin were *the* highlight of the whole trip. There are *five* of them, all in one little square; where else in the world ... ? I had a *marvellous* time cortège-ing out of one and into another and gazing at all those ikons and mosaics and murals and the absolute *forest* of golden onion domes and imagining I was the Grand Metropolitan on the set of *Boris Godunov* just about to crown the Tsar or make him confess to all sorts of *nameless* crimes; Jonathan in seventh *heaven* too, I mean these days ikons are his *thing*. And we saw the biggest dong (I mean bell) in the world : it sits on the pavement – too heavy to get it up. (The tower.) The Kremlin is quite *fabulous*.

Last time I shall write; we fly home tomorrow and when we see you will doubtless bore you into a *stupor* with all the details I haven't had space for in a letter *and* our colour slides *and* our babushka dolls; never mind, have got a *gigantic* bottle of vodka for you.

⋅ Home-counties ladies want us to visit them if we've ever in Coulsdon – no, they're *not*; they're widows, next-door neighbours – but Jonathan said (in private), 'Over our dead bodies.' Shan't be seeing the Yanks again either, or Burt and Agnes; they can all sink into Memory Lane, fly forgotten as a dream, ungathered rosebuds, ships that didn't (so to speak) go bump in the night. (I *adore* a good mixed metaphor) ... Life is so rich and varied and I do *enjoy* it!

Love and kisses from –
– The Grand Duchess Anastasia,
Tsaritsa of *All* the Russias. XXX

LOOKING FOR BORIS

One

They were going to live in Leningrad, and it was moving day. For weeks now Sasha, who was nine, and his brother Nikolai, who was six, had been thinking about the new flat. It was larger than their old one, and from the bedroom they were to share Sasha would be able to see the River Neva and all the splendours of the city – the Winter Palace, the Hermitage, St. Isaac's cathedral. Just the thought of it filled him with intense excitement.

But when the removal men started to take the furniture out and put it into the van, he was surprised to discover that he felt very upset. The bedroom, when the beds, the wardrobe and the carpet had gone, was bare and forlorn. I don't really want to leave, he said to himself. He looked out of the window and saw his friends playing on the grass. He would miss them.

His cat, Boris, a ginger tom, didn't like what was happening either. Boris slunk from room to room, sniffing and spitting. 'Don't worry,' Sasha said as he stroked him. 'There'll be lots of nice smells to enjoy in the new flat.' But Boris wouldn't be comforted. He began to shiver, and eventually curled himself up in a corner of one of the rooms, mewing softly.

'Sasha!' his mother called. 'Where are you? I need your help.'

He ran downstairs. The television was disconnected and standing in the middle of the kitchen floor. The fridge was empty, its door wide open. The table was covered with china and glass; Mum was wrapping cups and saucers in old newspapers and putting them in cardboard boxes.

'Help me with this,' she said, 'or we'll never get done in time.'

'Where's Dad?' Sasha asked.

'Outside with Nikolai, putting things into the car.'

It was a long job, but eventually all the china and glass was wrapped securely so it wouldn't break on the journey. 'I didn't realise we had so much stuff,' Sasha grumbled.

'Nor did I,' Mum answered. 'It's amazing what you collect over the years.'

While they worked, the removal men took everything out to the van – the chairs, the television, the fridge, the lampshades and the curtains. Last to go were the table and the cardboard boxes. The kitchen was now as forlorn as the other rooms.

'I'd like a glass of tea,' Sasha said.

'We can't. The kettle's packed and so are the glasses.'

Dad came in with Nikolai. 'All finished?' he asked. He looked round, approvingly. 'Good! Time to be off, then. I just hope we haven't left anything behind.'

They went out, locking the front door. 'Goodbye, old flat,' Sasha said. It hurt to think he would never go inside it again. All those memories! Mum put her arm round him and hugged him. So, he thought, she was feeling the same as he was: sad.

'It will be all right when we get to the new flat,' she said. 'You'll see! We'll enjoy ourselves deciding where to put everything.'

The removal men shut the van doors and drove off. 'We'll be quicker than them,' Dad said, as he and Mum and Sasha and Nikolai got into the car.

At the end of the road they turned left, and the flat was out of sight. I'm sure I've forgotten something, Sasha said to himself.

The journey was two hundred kilometres. His spirits lifted when he saw the spires and domes of Leningrad; it will be great, he thought, exploring the city. They reached the new flat only minutes ahead of the van. Mum had just unlocked the door when Sasha remembered what it was they'd left behind. 'Boris!' he shouted. 'He's still at home!'

'Oh, no!' Mum exclaimed. 'What on earth are we going to do?'

'You stay here,' Dad said. 'You can tell the men where to put the furniture. I'll drive back at once.'

'But ... what about the key? How will you get in?'

'We forgot something else,' Dad answered. 'Which is just as well. I should have given the key to the caretaker, but ... here it is! In my pocket.'

'I'll come too,' Sasha said. 'I can't bear to think of Boris all on his own! He'll be frightened to death!'

It was dark when they arrived at the old flat, which was empty, as the new people weren't moving in till the following day. The electricity was turned off, so they had to grope around with the help of the torch that was always kept in the car boot. It's creepy in here, Sasha said to himself; the walls are listening. Ghosts? He had never imagined before that there could be ghosts in the rooms where he lived. But, he thought, I have seen them again. This morning *wasn't* the last time.

Boris was still in the same place he had been when Mum called Sasha down to the kitchen. He was mewing pitifully, but after a moment or two he rubbed himself against Sasha's legs and began to purr. 'Come on!' Sasha said as he picked Boris up. 'Let's get out of here!'

Dad remembered to leave the key at the caretaker's this time. Boris did not enjoy the car ride. He lay on the floor under Sasha's seat, and refused to come out until they arrived at the new flat. 'How could we have forgotten you?' Sasha said. 'It's awful!'

Mum had supper waiting for them. Most of the furniture was in place, and several cardboard boxes had been unpacked.

'You've done well,' Dad said.

'I don't know if any of it is where we want it to be,' Mum answered.

Boris walked carefully from room to room, sniffing and purring. 'No harm done there,' Dad said. 'But fancy not remembering him!'

'Too much on our minds. Too many jobs to do.'

'I hope he'll forgive us,' Nikolai said, yawning. 'Ouf! Am I *weary*!'

In the boys' new room were the boxes with their possessions, the carpet and the wardrobe, and Mum had already hung up the curtains and made the beds. 'I'm going to like it here,' Sasha said to Nikolai, and he suddenly felt very cheerful. Boris was permitted to stay in their room that night, a privilege he usually did not have. Yes, Sasha thought, as he got undressed and put on his pyjamas, I really will like it here. But … what a day it's been!

Two

The first thing Sasha did when he got out of bed next morning was to run over to the window, open the curtains, and gaze out at the view. It was as marvellous as he'd imagined. There, beyond the wall on the other side of the street, sunlight danced on the River Neva, which was so wide here it was almost an estuary. In the distance was a bridge, and just next to it across the water was the Winter Palace, the home, before the Revolution, of the Tsars of Russia. He wanted to go inside the palace and see the magnificent tapestries, the paintings, the marble halls, the dazzling chandeliers.

He opened the window. It was a beautiful, hot May morning. People in the street below were in shirt-sleeves and summer dresses. But, because Leningrad was so far north, there were ice floes on the river: hundreds of them, like glittering white islands, floating swiftly down towards the Gulf of Finland, where they would eventually melt in the warm water of the sea.

At breakfast he asked, 'Can I go out?'

'Don't get yourself lost,' Dad said.

'I won't go far,' he promised.

Nikolai didn't want to come with him. He was more interested in the swings, the slide, and the roundabout in the park behind the flats. There was no such playground where they used to live. So Sasha strolled off on his own, and Mum and Dad went with Nikolai into the park, because he was too young to manage the swings by himself.

'More!' Nikolai shouted, as Dad pushed the swing. 'More! Send me right up into the air!'

'I'm tired out doing this,' Dad said. 'My arm muscles ache!'

The swing went slower and slower, even though Nikolai wriggled as hard as he could. Eventually it stopped. 'Why don't you try the roundabout?' Mum suggested. 'I'll come with you.'

'All right,' Nikolai answered. Soon he and Mum were whizzing round at top speed; Mum's long black hair streamed out behind her.

'I'm going on the slide!' Dad shouted. It was a splendid slide, painted blue and red, and it had a curve and a dip half-way up, so that it looked rather like a giant metal snake. Dad was a tall, powerfully built man, and very heavy. He shot down the slide and fell off the end, landing with a thump in the mud. 'It's a bit too slippery,' he said, as he stood up and felt himself for bruises. 'And my bottom's all wet!'

Nikolai and his mother roared with laughter.

'What a nuisance!' Dad grumbled. 'My jeans are covered in mud!'

'My turn for the slide,' Nikolai said. He was much less heavy than his father of course, so he came to a halt well before the end. Mum, too, was able to stop without falling off.

'It's fine for you two,' Dad said, and he walked away to have a go on the swings.

Nikolai loved the slide: he went on it again and again and again. Mum also enjoyed it, but she soon said, 'I've had enough!'

'I haven't,' Nikolai said.

'Well, take care. Each time we go on it, it seems to get more slippery. *I* nearly fell off, just now.' She walked across the park to Dad, and they both practised

31

on the swings, trying to beat each other at swinging higher.

'I can see St. Isaac's dome!' Mum yelled.

'But I'm higher than you are!' Dad shouted. 'I can see all the domes of Leningrad!'

Ten minutes later she said, 'We've lots to do. We haven't unpacked half our things yet.'

Dad nodded. 'All this exercise makes me thirsty. I fancy a glass of tea.' He called out to Nikolai, 'We're going home now!'

'One last time,' Nikolai called back as he ran up the steps of the slide. He slid down, head first. But too quickly: he fell off the end, clumsily, with a splat, in the mud. Mum and Dad hurried across to help him up.

'Another set of clothes for the wash,' Mum said. 'I don't think we'd better come here often! Did you hurt yourself?'

'I banged my knee.' He felt a bit dazed, and limped home in silence. While Mum boiled the kettle, and Dad opened one of the cardboard boxes, Nikolai pulled his favourite blue blanket off his bed, and took it into the living room. He curled up on the sofa with the blanket, and started to read a book.

'You didn't have that bad a fall,' Dad said.

'It still hurts.'

'Show me.' The left leg had swollen a little and was puffy just above the knee. It was painful when Dad touched it or tried to move it. 'Hmmm. We must keep an eye on that. But you'll probably be as right as rain by this evening.'

'Where's Boris gone? We left him in here.'

Dad looked round. 'I don't know,' he said.

Leningrad, Sasha thought, was a bit like cities in Western Europe. He had never been to Western Europe; it was almost impossibly difficult for Russians to travel abroad to countries such as England and France and Spain. But he had seen pictures of other parts of the world in books, and Leningrad reminded him of those pictures. It was like Venice, a city criss-crossed by canals. The canals were wider than those of Venice, and they had streets along their banks; but the houses and palaces had an Italian look about them. They were certainly quite unlike anything he had seen in Russia. And it was all so clean! Western cities, he had read, were dirty and full of litter, and in Venice the buildings were dilapidated and falling apart. Here, however, you could eat your dinner off the cobblestones, and the houses were well preserved and beautifully painted in soft pastel colours; green, yellow, brown, pink, blue.

He had learned a great deal about Leningrad in history lessons at school. Once upon a time it had been the capital of Russia, and it was the cradle of the October Revolution of 1917 which had ended the rule of the Tsars. The first shot had been fired from a ship, the *Aurora*, and there the ship still was, moored in the River Neva. As he walked across the square by the Admiralty Building, he pretended he was one of the huge crowd of rebels that had gathered here to storm the Winter Palace. Later, when he was inside the palace, he looked down from one of its windows and imagined he was the Tsar gazing out at the mob, wondering what to do with them. Then he remembered the Tsar had already been deposed and was in prison at that time; but no matter, he decided – he was somebody very important, the chief minister perhaps.

The Winter Palace was full of sightseers and tourists, many of them foreigners. Sasha overheard all sorts of languages, some of which he recognized – Finnish, Swedish, English, French. These people had come to see the marvels of the world's most famous museum. And there certainly were marvels to see – pillared halls of gold, tables made of a brilliant blue stone called lapis lazuli, enormous urns, pictures painted by the greatest painters ever known, and crystal chandeliers that glittered like stars. He was so enthralled he quite forgot how long he had been in there. When he did remember, he was amazed to see it was already half past two. That would mean trouble at home. He had missed his lunch, and Mum and Dad would be worried that he had got lost. When he turned up safe and sound, they would stop worrying and be angry instead.

He hurried out of the palace and sprinted down to the

river, then ran most of the way across the bridge and along the street that led to the flat.

When we got there, he discovered that neither of his parents was worried or angry, at least not with him. Two disasters had occurred since he went out that morning.

'Your brother has broken his leg,' Dad said. 'And Boris has disappeared off the face of the earth!'

Three

'We don't yet know if he *has* broken his leg,' Mum said. 'The doctor only said he might have done.'

Sasha stared at his brother: Nikolai was not careering about all over the place and getting into mischief as he usually did, but was sitting on the sofa, wrapped in his blue blanket and sucking his thumb. He looked very sorry for himself. 'What happened?' Sasha asked.

Mum and Dad explained. At first they'd told Nikolai not to be silly; he was inventing it, they said, because he was scared of going to his new school tomorrow. But as the morning wore on his knee began to throb and it swelled up. So they'd phoned a doctor, who told them to take him to the nearest hospital to have the leg X-rayed.

'But I shall look a right idiot,' Mum said, 'if there's nothing wrong with it!'

'Haven't you been to the hospital yet?' Sasha asked.

'I'm just about to go ... we were waiting for you to return.'

'Do you want me to help?'

'You can look for the cat,' Dad said. 'He must have got out when I left the front door open. I'm going to find the park-keeper and complain about the slide. Some other kid might break his bones on it. Or his neck.'

'Or *her* bones, or *her* neck,' Mum said.

'After that ... I'll cook us some dinner.'

'Ugh!' Sasha said. 'That means we'll all be poisoned!' He stepped nimbly aside as Dad aimed a friendly clout at him.

'Go and look for Boris,' Dad said. 'He can't have gone far.'

At the casualty department of the hospital, Nikolai and Mum had to wait a long time, but when it was their turn to be seen, the doctor and the nurses were pleasant and helpful.

'Will there be any pain?' Nikolai asked, when he saw the X-ray machine.

'Pain?' the doctor echoed. 'Certainly not! This machine is a camera. X-rays are photographs; we shall take some pictures of your bones, to find out what damage has been done.'

'How can you do that? You can't see my bones.'

The doctor laughed. 'Oh, yes we can!' he said. 'And you can see them too, when the X-rays are developed.'

After the pictures were taken, there was another long wait, but eventually Nikolai found himself staring at some gigantic photographs. 'Is that really the inside of my leg?' he asked. 'Doesn't it look peculiar!'

'A bit more peculiar than it should look,' the doctor said. 'That line there, that's a fracture, a break. Children's bones don't snap in half as adults' bones sometimes do, but they may get chipped or cracked. You've got a cracked bone, just above your knee.'

'Nikolai ... I'm so sorry I didn't believe you!' Mum said.

'That leg has got to be covered in plaster from the thigh to the ankle,' the doctor went on. 'Don't worry,' he said, seeing the expression on Nikolai's face. 'It won't hurt at all, but you'll probably get a bit fed up with it, because I want you to wear it for a month. It takes that long for the bone to heal. We'll give you some crutches so you can hobble about. And be warned – you'll have to come back here for the whole thing to be plastered over again if you get it wet. It goes soggy in water.'

'But ... how will I have a shower?'

The doctor smiled. 'With difficulty,' he said.

The park-keeper, an old, purple-faced man, listened to

Dad's story, then he said, 'Harrumph! Let's go and have a look at the slide.'

It was late in the afternoon; school had finished for the day, and dozens of children were enjoying themselves on the roundabout, the slide, and the swings. Dad and the park-keeper watched. 'They shoot down much too quickly,' Dad said. 'It's dangerous!'

The park-keeper grunted. A very tall, very fat boy climbed the steps to the top of the slide: he whizzed down with the speed of a rocket, and fell off the end, into the mud. But he wasn't hurt; he stood up and laughed. Then it was the turn of one of the girls. She shot down, screaming, her dress billowing high in the air. She, too, fell off, and like the fat boy she scrambled to her feet and laughed.

'They don't seem to be crippling themselves,' the park-keeper said.

'I could complain to the City Council,' Dad said.

'Oh you could, could you?'

'Yes. I could.'

The park-keeper glared at him for a long moment. Then he fished around in his jacket, and pulled out a rouble. 'Buy your kid some chocolate,' he said.

Dad didn't accept the bribe. 'I could complain,' he repeated. The park-keeper glared at him a second time, and muttered something incomprehensible.

On Wednesday afternoon that week a gang of men came into the park, dismantled the slide, and took it away.

Sasha began his search by ringing the bells of all the flats on the floors above his own, but nobody upstairs had seen Boris. He then tried the downstairs flats, and obtained the same reply. There was one more bell, on the ground floor. It was the first piece of luck: the old woman who answered the ring said, yes, she had seen a ginger cat about two hours ago. He'd walked out onto the pavement, then over the street, using the pedestrian crossing.

'Just like a person waiting for the traffic to clear,' she said. 'Very amusing, I thought.'

'That sounds like Boris,' Sasha said. 'He's an extremely smart cat.'

'Are you the new people upstairs?'

'Yes.'

'I hope you're settling in all right.'

'We've lost our cat and my brother has broken his leg.'

'Troubles never come singly,' the old woman said.

'Which way did Boris go when he got to the other side of the street?'

'To the left, I think. Yes, to the left. Towards the bridge.'

'Thank you.'

There were a great many tour buses parked by the bridge, and hundreds of sightseers leaning on the wall, taking photographs of the ice floes and the Winter Palace. It was one of the most popular views in Leningrad. But, Sasha said to himself, none of these people would have been here two hours ago, so it was pointless asking them. Who *could* he ask? There was a kiosk nearby that sold tea and soft drinks, but the enormous queue of men, women and children waiting to be served discouraged him. A little further on was the entrance to a metro station: perhaps Boris had gone in there. A policeman stood by its doors.

'Have you seen a ginger cat?' Sasha asked.

'Yes,' the policeman said. 'He went into the metro station. I tried to shoo him out, but he wouldn't come.'

'Do you think he could have gone down to the trains?'

The policeman shrugged his shoulders. 'I've no idea,' he said.

Sasha had never travelled on a metro before. He didn't even know how to buy a ticket. So he watched what other people were doing; it was the rush hour, and thousands of Leningrad's inhabitants were going home from work. You didn't need a ticket, he discovered: all you had to do was put a five copeck coin in a slot machine, then walk through a barrier. It was easy! So he did the same as everybody else, and found he was on an escalator that plunged downwards at high speed and was so long he couldn't see the bottom of it. Boris would never have ventured onto this, he thought – he would have been too frightened.

On the platforms hordes of people were milling about, pushing and shoving to get in and out of trains. Not many passengers spoke to one another; they were too intent on arriving at their destinations as quickly as possible. The air smelled fusty, and the lighting was dim. There was no sign of Boris. Sasha felt depressed and unwanted: the crowds of people made him realise how vast the city was, and impersonal, as if nobody really cared about other human beings, let alone cats.

He struggled through to the up escalator. Soon he was out of the station, in the street and the early evening sunlight. It was quieter here, and the air tasted good. The river gurgled happily, and the Winter Palace on the opposite bank seemed to nod at him, as if recognizing someone it had met before.

The buses had all gone, carrying the sightseers to their hotels for dinner. There was no queue now at the soft drinks kiosk, but it was still open. Inside it, looking rather bored, was a boy of about Sasha's age.

'I've lost my cat,' Sasha said. 'I wondered if you'd seen him.'

'A ginger cat?'

'Yes! Where is he?'

The boy laughed. 'A long way away from here! He leaped onto one of the tour buses.'

Sasha gasped with horror. 'Oh, no! Then we've lost him for good!'

'Not necessarily. I saw where the bus was going. The Kirov Theatre.'

'Where's that?'

The boy stared at Sasha in surprise. 'Everyone knows the Kirov! It's the most famous theatre in all Russia!'

'We've only just moved to Leningrad,' Sasha said. 'Yesterday.'

'Ah.' The boy's voice sounded a bit kinder. 'Tell you what ... I'm only looking after this place while my Dad has his tea. If you come back here at seven o'clock I'll help you look for your cat. I've nothing else to do this evening. What's his name?'

'Boris.'

'And yours?'

'Sasha.'

'I'm Kolya. Have a drink … an orange juice. On the house.'

'Well, that's … thank you very much.'

They smiled at each other. Kolya's eyes were blue, and they seemed warm and trusting. I might have lost a cat, Sasha said to himself, but I may have found a friend.

Four

When Sasha got home, Mum and Nikolai had just returned from the hospital. Nikolai had recovered all his energies: the pain had gone, and he treated the plastered leg as if it was a new toy. 'Sasha! You'll have to give me more respect now!' he cried. 'One clump from this and I could knock you out cold!'

'You'd need an army to do that,' Sasha replied.

Nikolai whirled one of the crutches round, above his head, as if it was a lassoo. Then he fell over. He needed help from Sasha to get up, and for a few minutes he was rather quiet, sitting on a chair with a thoughtful expression on his face. But he rallied quickly and was off again, stumping round the room at an impressively fast speed.

Mum sighed. 'I think we're in for a reign of terror these next four weeks,' she said. 'What am I going to do with him?'

'Dinner's ready!' Dad shouted from the kitchen. 'Everybody sit at the table!'

'Did you find Boris?' Mum asked.

'No.' Sasha related the story of his search, and said he was meeting Kolya at seven to go to the Kirov.

'Well … a cat hunt's one way of getting to know a new city! Sasha … I don't think we should worry ourselves too much about Boris. Not yet. He'll turn up. Cats don't like moving, even less than humans do. If he did jump on that bus, he's probably still there, hiding under a seat.'

Sasha was not convinced. 'Cats sometimes *hate* their new homes. They try and return to their old ones; they've been known to walk hundreds of miles.'

'He'll stroll in here when he wants some food. You'll see.'

Dinner, a beetroot salad followed by pork casserole, was much better than Sasha had imagined it would be. 'You should do this more often,' he said to his father.

'About time my children learned to cook,' Dad replied.

'What? With Mum *and* you to do it for us?'

'Suppose you marry a wife who can't even make a cup of coffee?'

'Sasha married!' Nikolai exclaimed. 'No decent girl would look at him once!'

'Can I go out now?' Sasha asked.

'Yes,' Mum said. She squeezed his hand affectionately. She knew that he was, deep down, really very worried about Boris. 'I bet you he's still on that bus, and you'll find the bus parked by the Kirov, waiting for the people to come out when the opera has finished.'

'They do opera at the Kirov?' Nikolai asked. He warbled a few tuneless notes.

'And ballet,' Dad said.

There were twenty tour buses outside the theatre. The drivers were snoozing, or reading magazines, or just staring blankly at nothing in particular; they all looked as if time was passing very slowly. 'I didn't realise there'd be such a lot of them,' Sasha said.

'We'll have to search every one,' Kolya answered.

There was no cat, ginger or otherwise, in any of the buses, and none of the drivers had noticed Boris getting on board at the place where the tourists photographed the Neva and the Winter Palace.

'But I saw him!' Kolya said. 'I know I haven't made a mistake!'

'Do you think he's gone into the theatre?' Sasha suggested.

Kolya seemed doubtful. 'But we could look,' he said. 'Why not?'

'Will they let us in?'

There was no one to stop them. The performance – a ballet, *The Sleeping Princess* by Tchaikovsky – had started three quarters of an hour ago, and the doormen had gone off duty, as had the programme sellers and the women who checked the tickets. The foyer of the theatre was empty. 'Come on!' Kolya said. 'Let's explore this place while we have the chance! I've never been in here.'

'We'll get into trouble.'

'Chicken?'

'No!'

They climbed up staircases and tiptoed along corridors, avoiding the bar where people were preparing drinks for the interval. Eventually they found themselves in a narrow passageway behind the dress circle. A small door stood open, and beyond it were chairs and a view of the stage, which was filled with dancers.

'This is one of the boxes, I guess,' Kolya said. 'And there's nobody in it. Shall we sit down and see what's going on?'

'Do you think we should?'

'Who is there to say we shouldn't?'

The orchestra was directly beneath them. It was dark down there, except for the lights on the players' desks which lit up the copies of the music, the musicians' heads, and the rich gleaming brown of their instruments. It's like some old painting in the Winter Palace, Sasha said to himself. The orchestra was playing *The Sleeping Princess* waltz. He had heard this piece, and he hummed it in time to the music.

'Ssh!' Kolya said.

It was the Princess's eighteenth birthday. The scene was a wood in summer; the royal family was holding a party – an outdoor picnic – and friends and relatives were offering all kinds of gifts. The dancing was lively, joyous; the music happy and full of energy. Then the wicked fairy appeared and gave the Princess a needle. She pricked her finger. The music changed, and all the dancing stopped. Everyone present, apart from the fairy, was frozen in sleep for the next hundred years. The curtain came down; the audience applauded wildly, and the house lights began

41

to shine. It was the interval. Sasha, for a moment, had forgotten Boris. What he had just seen and heard he thought was the most exciting and beautiful thing he had ever experienced.

'Are we going to stay for the rest of it?' Kolya asked.

'What time does it finish?'

'I don't know … ten o'clock, perhaps.'

'I'll be in real trouble if I'm out that late.'

'Me too. I suppose we ought to go.'

'Yes. Anyway … Boris isn't here.'

They walked back through the twilit streets, parting at the end of the bridge across the Neva. 'See you tomorrow,' Kolya said. 'Come over to the kiosk after school. You could help me to sell some drinks, if you like.'

'I'd love to!' Sasha said. 'And maybe we'll have another adventure.'

'What school will you be going to?' Kolya asked.

'I'm not sure of its name.'

'Probably my school. That would be great!'

Sasha watched him walk off into the darkness. Life in Leningrad would be terrific, he thought, if only … if only he could find that cat!

Five

Mum and Dad had more trouble with Nikolai's broken leg than he did himself. They had to carry him down the stairs to the street, help him dress and undress, and make sure the leg stayed dry when he was in the shower. 'It's all quite exhausting!' Mum said. On one occasion in the bathroom, the plaster got wet, and though Dad dried it at once, it was too late; it went soft. So Nikolai had a morning off school; Mum drove him to the hospital once again, and the doctor removed the soggy, useless plaster. Nikolai could see his leg for the first time since he broke it – it looked thin and pale, but at least it wasn't swollen now.

'It's doing just fine,' the doctor said, as he covered the leg in fresh plaster.

At his new school, the children wanted to borrow one, or both, of his crutches at play-time for games of wounded sailors and injured soldiers; Nikolai enjoyed himself deciding whose turn it should be to have them. His teacher, Miss Bulgakov, made him sit at the front of the room, the broken leg resting on a chair. 'I shall be the first to autograph it,' she said, and she wrote her name on it in green ink. The children wanted to write their names on it too, so Nikolai had a complete list of his class-mates' signatures on his leg. On the day after he'd gone to the hospital for the second time, the names had to be written out again on the new plaster.

His knee didn't hurt at all now. It was annoying, of course, having this ugly, heavy, thick casing to drag around, and he couldn't run and dash everywhere as he usually did. The skin inside sometimes itched, and he wanted to scratch it. That was impossible, but it didn't worry him a great deal. He was looking forward to the day when the plaster would be cut off; but, he decided, breaking a limb wasn't such a horrible experience as he had imagined. It had also turned out to be a very worthwhile introduction to his new school. Instead of being ignored, or teased as 'the new boy', he had got sympathy and been the centre of attention. He liked that.

Sasha had no problem either, settling into the new school, though the first days of finding out where everything was – his classroom, the gym, the hall and so on – were bewildering. Work was not much different from his old school, and it wasn't too awful adjusting to the places the class had got to in its lessons; in some subjects he was ahead of the other children, in some merely a bit behind. His friendship with Kolya was a great help. Kolya was not only at the same school; he was in the same class.

When school was over for the day, Sasha sometimes worked with him in the soft drinks kiosk and earned himself a little pocket money. At other times he wandered about the city, looking for Boris. He began to know the streets and canals and buildings better than Dad and Mum did. It was June, a marvellous month to be out of doors in Leningrad, that hot period of the year called 'White Nights': the ice floes have all melted; the sun never sets, and even when it is low over the horizon at twelve o'clock midnight, you can still read a book without switching on a lamp.

He thought he had found Boris on two occasions. He spotted a hungry ginger tom eating a fish head in the street by the Finland Station, but he soon realised this cat didn't look anything like Boris. One evening he went to visit Leningrad's war memorial. The city had been besieged by the Germans in the Great Patriotic War for nine hundred days – it was the longest siege in all history. Nearly a million people had starved to death. While Sasha was reading about it in the little museum under the memorial, he felt a furry body rubbing against his legs. He looked down: a ginger cat! But it wasn't Boris.

'We have to get used to the idea that he may have disappeared for good,' Dad said. 'He got himself lost, and someone found him and took him in. Adopted him.'

'Perhaps we ought to think about having another cat,' Nikolai said.

'No!' Sasha cried. Boris wasn't just any old cat; he was – Boris. Sasha couldn't recall a time when Boris hadn't been a part of his life. They were the same age. His earliest memories were of a ginger kitten pouncing on a toy mouse, then, when he started school, he would talk to Boris when he got home and tell him the day's events. Boris listened. Or, as least, purred.

Dad looked at Mum. Mum looked at Dad. They didn't say anything.

Four weeks after his accident, Mum took Nikolai to the hospital to have his leg X-rayed again. It was another morning off school. 'Fine,' the doctor said, when he'd studied the photographs. 'Just fine! It's healed really well.' So the plaster was slit from top to bottom, but the process of removing it caused it to break in several pieces. Nikolai was disappointed. He'd wanted to take it home as a souvenir as it had his friends' signatures on it. 'Never mind,' the doctor said. 'Just tell yourself your knee is now as perfect as before you fractured it. That's good, don't you think?'

'Yes,' Nikolai answered.

'But you'll have to learn how to walk.'

'I know how to walk!'

'You haven't used any of those muscles for weeks. They'll get tired very quickly.'

The doctor was right, Nikolai discovered. After half an hour his bones ached; he felt as if he'd been climbing mountains. 'It hurt less when I had the plaster *on*,' he grumbled. But each day he could go a little further before he got tired; and, after a fortnight, it was as if he had never broken his leg at all. He was running about everywhere, and playing football again.

The City Council put a new slide in the park. It wasn't as big as the old one, and it didn't have a curve and a dip it it. Nor was it painted bright red and blue; it was a dull, uninteresting brown. But it was safe. There were no more accidents.

Six

Sasha and Kolya were walking along the bank of the canal that led to the Redemption Church. They were discussing whether it would be possible, in the future, to build aeroplanes that went faster than the fastest supersonic jets already in existence.

'One day,' Kolya said, 'we'll have a plane that travels at the speed of light.'

'It wouldn't be much use,' Sasha answered.

'Why not?'

'If it flew at the speed of light, you wouldn't be able to see it.'

'You mean everyone on board would be invisible?'

'This is a daft conversation,' Sasha said.

They stopped walking, and gazed at the Redemption

Church. It was covered in scaffolding as it was being repaired and redecorated, but it was, nonetheless, an impressive sight. Its roof was a forest of huge towers, and on top of each tower was an onion-shaped dome. Some of these domes were painted gold; others had patterns – zigzags, diamonds, crescents, squares – in all kinds of vivid colours: scarlet, pea green, azure blue, purple.

'They look like enormous hats,' Kolya said.

'There're supposed to look like hats. The builders, in the Middle Ages, designed them as copies of soldiers' helmets.'

'How do you know?'

'You never listen to anything in class! Our teacher told us ... oh, on Thursday.'

'They're beautiful,' Kolya said.

'Yes. They are.'

They stared up for a while in silence. 'There's something moving around on the top of that gold dome,' Kolya said. 'Look! The smallest one on the left. What is it? It isn't a bird. It's ...'

'It's a cat! I can see it now. A ginger cat! Boris!'

'Yes! It is a ginger cat! But you can't tell from this distance whether it's Boris or not. How on earth did it get there?'

'What are we going to do?'

'We couldn't climb up to him; it's far too dangerous. And somebody would stop us, or call the police. Let's see if there's anyone in the church.'

But the church, which was a museum nowadays, had shut at five o'clock, and the men who were repairing its outside had gone home. There was only one thing to do: they would have to call the fire brigade. Firemen had ladders that were long enough to reach up that high. The man who answered the phone said they would come as soon as they could, but it might be a while: it wasn't an emergency. He asked for Kolya's and Sasha's names and addresses, then he said, 'If this is a practical joke, I'll have you arrested as juvenile delinquents. You could get sent to Siberia.'

46

'That's rubbish!' Sasha said, angrily. 'And it is *not* a practical joke!'

'Wait outside the church. We'll be at least half an hour.'

They spent the time watching the cat. It was too far away for them to hear if it was mewing, but it looked as if it was in a state of considerable distress. It prowled around on the top of the dome, trying to find a point where it could jump, but whenever it thought it had found one it lost its nerve and scurried back to safety.

The firemen arrived. Sasha had assumed they would climb the scaffolding up to the dome, but they didn't; they used a ladder, an immense thing that operated hydraulically. 'The biggest we've got,' one of them said. Indeed it was so big it could have gone up much higher, at least as far as the next dome.

The platform at the top of the ladder came to rest against the side of the dome, but it was still some way away from the cat; and the fireman who stood on it had a very difficult job persuading the cat to move down to him. A large crowd began to assemble, wanting to know what was going on. A cat, people said, up on the dome. Incredible! Unheard of! Whatever next!

'That fireman must be very brave,' Kolya said. 'I can't bear heights!'

The cat, realising that somebody was trying to rescue it, eventually half-walked, half-skidded down the side of the dome into the fireman's waiting arms. The ladder was quickly lowered, and the fireman – and the cat – reached the ground.

Sasha pushed his way through the people. 'Boris!' he yelled.

Mangy, dirty, starving and bewildered, Boris – it *was* he – sprang from the fireman's grip onto Sasha's shoulder.

'Is he yours?' the fireman asked.

'Yes. Am I pleased to see him!'

'You should take more care of your animals. We can't waste all our time going round Leningrad rescuing cats! If we did, everybody would get burned to a cinder!'

'It wasn't my fault,' Sasha said.

'Well … no harm done. But don't let him do it again!'

Sasha and Kolya had some difficulty getting through the crowd. People wanted to see Boris, stroke him, say a few words to him; but eventually they lost interest, and the two boys could make their way home.

'So this is Boris,' Kolya said. He shook one of the cat's paws. 'I'm very pleased to meet you. I've heard so much about you!'

'It's marvellous!' Sasha cried. 'Wonderful!' And, to himself, he said: now I can *really* begin to enjoy Leningrad!

Next day Mum, Dad, Sasha and Nikolai went into the park. 'Let's have a go on the new slide,' Dad said.

'We shouldn't,' said Mum. 'We're adults.'

'That didn't stop you before.'

So they all slid down the slide, and said that though it wasn't dangerous it was not as exciting as the old one; they whizzed round on the roundabout, laughing and shouting and screaming; then they raced over to the swings.

'Sasha, you'll have to push me,' Nikolai said.

'No,' Sasha answered. 'You can do it yourself if you try hard enough.'

'I can't.'

'Yes, you can.'

He found he could. It was just a matter of kicking his legs out at exactly the right moment. 'I can do it!' he said. 'I can *do* it!'

The four swings rocked backwards and forwards together, higher and higher. 'I can see St. Isaac's dome!' Mum shouted.

'I can see all the domes!' Dad yelled. 'I'm the highest!'

'I can see St. Isaac's too!' Nikolai shrieked. Then he said, enviously, 'I'll never be able to swing as high as Dad.'

'Oh yes, you will!'

'I'm dizzy,' said Mum. The swings got slower and slower, then stopped. Mum and Dad and Sasha and Nikolai were laughing, panting for breath, their eyes shining.

'That was fun,' Sasha said.

'Time for tea,' Dad announced. 'And cake.'

'I've learned to *swing*!' Nikolai said. 'Better than slippery old slides any day of the week!'

'There's Boris.' Boris had followed them into the park. He was painfully thin, but his fur was already much cleaner. He was walking delicately through the flower beds, sniffing at the blossom.

'How did he survive?' Mum asked. 'Where did he live?'

'We'll never find out,' Dad answered. 'Go and get him, Sasha. We can't have him straying off again.'

Boris was more than willing to be picked up: he began to purr, immediately. 'You've come back,' Sasha said, stroking him. 'That's what *really* counts!'

Sasha and Kolya leaned on the river wall, arms round each other's shoulders, and gazed at the palace on the opposite bank. 'You are an old softy,' Kolya said. 'You and that cat! But I like you ... just as you are.'

'I like you too,' Sasha answered, and he stroked Kolya's ear.

'I'm pleased your mum said you could stay overnight at our place ... it gets boring, being an only child. Are you sure you won't get cat-sick?'

'Cat-sick?'

'Pining for Boris.'

'Of course not!'

'Let's go home now ... I've so many things to show you!'

BRIDFORD

Remember that foggy, bleak New Year's Day
A detective inspector called, wanting
To buy our house? In bed at tea-time.
'At it again!' our neighbours often said.
You went to the door in my dressing-gown,
Erect as a tent. He, we guessed, had guessed.
I, draped only in a quilt, held court,
Haggling prices. He laughed – and bought.

Icy January day: we quarrelled – you,
In expected ill-temper, were driving
Too fast. The car skidded dizzily,
Wildly spinning, and then: a miracle: it
Stopped. We were almost speechless. Later,
We fell into bed, and fucked and fucked and
Fucked, never so needing one another –
Never before had death clutched us.

On motorways at seventy miles an hour,
Against walls, upside down on staircases,
Hendon High Street at four p.m. as
Suburban women shopped. And frequently
When I was washing up, a plate in each
Wet soapy hand, tempted to clout you while
You sucked. Once I yelled 'Rape!' and the lodgers
Quietly shut their bedroom doors.

In quality, quantity, we explored
The whole gamut. Boring if one of
Us did not want it: fun: ridiculous:

Sensually slow: a quick athletic screw:
KY, nothing, or head to foot in oil:
At times, so utterly complete it was
Like being face to face with God. Do you
Now find such love with anyone? I don't.

EXETER

I can remember words in sleep
Mattress on the floor
You touching me in sleep
September morning light
September of golden rod
Wrapped in a blanket.

I can remember listening to music
Curled in a chair
You in a younger bed
Grey October dawn
October of poison ivy
Wrapped in sour berries.

I can remember violence of feelings
Knife in my hand
You touching him in sleep
September morning light
September of purple love-lies-bleeding
I slashed your car tyres.

I can remember the sweet aftermath
Love-making on the floor
You touching me in sleep
Golden October dawn
October of dying kingcups
Wrapped in evasions, lies.

TORQUAY

On summer nights, wall-to-wall men:
Armpits, a hundred sweet-sour aftershaves.
Too small for a real disco. The juke-box
Still plays *First Time Ever I Saw Your Face*,
When Will I See You Again? England's smallest.

You never liked it much. Or so
You said – in my absence you often went.
First time ever I saw your face was there;
Really saw it, I mean; first time ever
I danced with you was there. First time.

Remember that stranger, a shy
Elderly man who bought us drinks? He said
He'd never seen two people so in love
With one another as we were. Later,
On one hot night, your heavy wooden clogs

Kicked me all over that postage-stamp
Dance floor, because on no grounds at all you
Said I did not love you. I remember
Being in your arms, the salt sweat of your face
On mine and kisses, loving you so much too

Much. Yes, Torquay's a seedy town,
Not what it was; the old ladies have gone
Elsewhere. Too many clubs and fish and chips
And murders, but for me it only has
Our story. Now other bodies press mine on

That miniscule floor; if I go
To bed with them it's always sweet-sour sex,
No precious moments, and I don't recall
First time ever I saw them: your ghost slips
In between.

CROCKERNWELL

Remember the cottage I bought for us,
Thatch, log fires, old beams, white walls? – it was an idyll.
You never really wanted it.
You came because you had no other place to go:
Enjoyed yourself arranging it as you
Thought fit, a beautiful back-drop just right
For holding elegant dinner parties,
Not something to be worked for, earned. You thought
I should have given you half, American
Holiday, car, tossed in like Green Shield stamps.
You'd lie in bed till noon, then watch TV
Until the programmes finished, and you'd say
That life was hard, not worth a candle. Huh!
Delicately pruning the sick roses
Was your idea of help in the garden.
Small wonder that I spent the days and months
Stomach churning, sour with annoyances.

It's true you cooked some first-class meals, and bought
The occasional bag of groceries,
A ballet ticket, a TV licence.

Time to move on, you told yourself, high time!
A cat you said you loved the day you went
Knew what was happening, but your eyes were dry.
You told me in mid-winter. Another
Christmas alone! How well you always wrecked
Christmas! Almost sadistically (some
Friends would say it was sadistically),
One in two, as regular as clockwork.

Each spoiled season meant a new house. I think
You'll always be remembered as the man
Who loved to decorate his boyfriends' rooms
And then abandoned them: like used tissues.

CUBE HOUSES

Travellers' tales are exaggerations; half the fun of exploring a new city is rubbing off myth and seeing reality. 'In Ethiopia,' Sir John Mandeville said, 'there are many diverse people, and Ethiopia is called Cusis. In that country the people have only one foot, but they hop so quickly that it is a marvel; and the foot is so large that when they lie down and rest it shades the whole of the body from the sun.' So, a tourist in the fourteenth century. San Francisco, we are told, was destroyed in an earthquake, and Hitler's planes smashed Rotterdam to pieces. I assumed, as I stared at the beautiful Victorian houses on Diamond and Douglass, that they were rebuilt after 1906. In fact the earthquake didn't touch them; only the business quarter – downtown – was ruined. Rotterdam, I discover, is for the most part pleasantly nineteenth century too. The German bombs in 1940 flattened only some of it.

I am here for a writers' conference, perhaps the largest gathering of gay and lesbian wordsmiths Europe has ever seen. There are hundreds of them. I'm not well, have not been well for over a month, and therefore I'm depressed and rather vulnerable. Back problems that reduce my walk to a hobble (there's something wrong with a joint connecting the pelvis to the spine); a loose tooth, an abscess and gum recession; indigestion almost every day. Antibiotics for the abscess, anti-inflammatory drugs for the back, Altacite for the stomach – the combination of the three makes me nauseous. I can't even enjoy a beer or a glass of wine.

I need tender company, but old acquaintances are too busy amusing themselves. 'When you're ill,' Tom

Wakefield says, 'no one is particularly sympathetic.'
And laughs – I can't tell if sympathetically or not. A
week of people coming up to me and asking, 'Have
you seen X or Y?' And when I've answered they hurry
away, clutching books and papers and clip-boards like
Chaucer's sergeant-at-law – 'And yet he semed bisier than
he was.' I feel unwanted too, in a professional capacity.
Nobody's asked me to do anything much, merely speak
on an obscure panel with five Dutch children's writers (in
an obscure room to an audience of maybe twenty souls);
the chairperson doesn't even bother to contact me until
moments before we start. It is *not* a success. That evening a
group of British writers address the whole conference, but
I haven't been invited to stick in my tuppence worth. They
talk a lot about Clause 28; the two books I seem to recollect
(how could I not?) that were singled out for vilification
by the morality jerks in Parliament were *Jenny Lives With
Eric and Martin* and *The Milkman's On His Way*, but neither
is mentioned. *The Milkman's* author, I want to shout, is
here; his view of the matter might be of interest. He's had
thirty-five books published and has won two literary prizes.
Passes scrutiny, has been given clearance.

I'm not usually such a sulking prima donna. In fact I
don't think I'm a prima donna at all. But illness and pain
affect the mind, the whole man. I remember the slogans
on the Clause 28 marches: 'Proust and Oscar Wilde will
be chucked out of our libraries and schools!' A nonsense,
a dangerous nonsense – because it's so patently untrue
– and the banner-wavers knew it. Not one banner said,
'Hands off *The Milkman*!' Not one person or organization spoke up; indeed, they seemed to be positively
dissociating themselves from it.

I like the trams, their yellow eyes probing the dark these
misty October nights; the canals, silent and still, along the
centres of roads, the detritus of autumn floating on their
surfaces; the colour of trees ... Delfshaven – its barges
and house-boats, old waterside dwellings picturesquely
propping one another up, its windmill you can visit free:
scent of old wood; dry, dusty smells of flour and sacks;

new bread, croissants, cakes (the downstairs is a coffee shop.) I enjoy, despite the constant pain in my spine and right thigh, my ability to get myself there: give me, in any strange city, a map of the streets and the metro system, and I'm off, exploring, usually happy as a sand-kid …

Ten a.m., and I'm with a small group of either devotees or the merely curious listening to an intelligent, well-researched paper on vampires. Vampires as a gay image, a gay metaphor. Can't see much likeness myself, except the it-takes-one-to-know-one syndrome. What extraordinary things we talk about! How we love to extend being gay into every department of existence! What absurdities it brings us to! All reality, one speaker said yesterday, is heterosexual. And another asked Maureen Duffy to comment on the parallels between her campaigning for animal rights and gay and lesbian sensibility. Maureen extricated herself with some nimble foot-work; she is impressive – good writers do not often speak as well as she does. We've never met and I'd like to be introduced, but nobody offers. I can't go up to someone and say 'Hi, I'm … '

A vampire story is an interesting challenge, but Bram Stoker (heterosexual reality?) did it so superbly I'm sure I couldn't get away from the shadow of *Dracula*. I'm thinking about this as I leave the room, and I nearly bump into a very tall, very thin person – man? Woman? Trans-sexual? For a moment vampires are a *homosexual* reality …

The barman in the Mateloos has been doing his job for less than a week, but already he's more efficient than many thoroughly experienced bar persons in Britain. He's friendly, twenty-two years old, and extremely cute. He lives with his lover, and gets on well, he says, with his 'mother-in-law.' Tomorrow is his birthday; he and the lover will be dining out with both sets of parents, who strongly approve of the relationship. Mothers-in-law, I observe, can sometimes be difficult. 'Oh, I've plenty of experience,' he answers. 'I've had ten.' He grins. 'I've not been a good boy.'

So unlike the home life of this dear queen …

If it weren't for the kindness of my host I would probably be eating in solitude every night. He is a writer and I'm staying in his flat; he has a lover of some twenty years' standing, who lives just round the corner. They share most things including their evening meal, but not the bedroom: sex ended long ago, and as they travel their own ways in the bars (my host is pursuing a Moroccan youth who so far hasn't succumbed) they feel they need tangible signs of separate existence. Night owls; they don't return from the bars till six a.m., seven a.m. A peculiar way to live at forty-five years of age. I couldn't do it. I wouldn't want to do it.

Kind, as I said, but not people I've warmed to. In my host's kitchen there are unwashed pans with luxuriant moulds taking root, and the lover's flat reeks of cat piss. (The hi fi, however, is splendid and I much enjoy hearing the Brahms B flat concerto.) At dinner one night, my stomach nauseous – from my medications, not the food – I have a rare freak-out about AIDS. Below par for more than a month now; has the virus begun to do its dirty work? When I'm back in England, will I be shut away in a bedroom, a hospital? A few moments of real fear.

I need to talk to someone about this, but the conference persons wouldn't wish their happy, busy week thus interrupted. There's nobody at home I can talk to about it either, not one of my friends. They all know I've been HIV positive for four years; they've all expressed concern and sympathy and affection. But not one of them wants to understand what I feel – the chance that I may (when? soon?) be ill, dying, dead, they find too disturbing to contemplate. Which is flattering, I suppose. But no comfort. So I've given up talking about it except when I absolutely must.

I test the ground with Joe Mills at a conference party one evening and say most people tell me to look on the bright side ... it may never happen ... think of the books I still have to write ... This isn't what I want to hear, I explain, any more than its opposite ('Poor thing! How *awful* it must be!'); what I do want – and don't get – is a sympathetic mail-box where I can post my black thoughts. Dead letters.

Joe says, with a laugh – a rueful laugh? – that he was going to tell me to look on the bright side … it may never …

So I change the subject immediately.

Peter Burton on Christopher Isherwood is another intelligent, carefully researched paper; though I don't in fact learn anything new I'm stimulated and I enjoy it. He's in a happy mood this week, knocking back the odd glass of Pernod and wearing his abroad outfit, which includes a Breton onion-man beret worn at a rakish angle; he looks like an able seaman who's accidentally strolled in from Rotterdam port. Some good moments gossiping with him in the Mateloos …

Tom's session is supposed to be on the relationship between autobiography and fiction; it's in fact Tom on Tom: first-class entertainment and none the worse for that, even if it isn't easy to judge where the autobiography ends and the fiction begins. 'My mother died at forty-one … all working-class women did in those days, you see;' later, 'She died at fifty-one … all working-class women died before they were sixty.' I think of Grandma Rees, parlourmaid in rural, nineteenth-century Norfolk, then nursemaid at the British Embassy in Paris, then wife to a London tram-driver; she died of cancer at seventy-two. But it's small-minded of me to carp. Tom in full spate gives a great deal of himself, and the result is fun, and worthwhile, and we know a little better the character he wants us to know, which is the character we sense between the words in his books. It's a clever way of continuing to be the invisible man.

If he had the virus he wouldn't increase another's burdens by disclosing his thoughts on the subject. I envy that.

I limp round the Boymans Museum, not the world's finest art gallery, but nevertheless interesting, with at least one good example of most of the major painters. A wealth of Dutch landscapes, battles at sea, interiors, portraits; none of them at all bad or indifferent. Two unusual Sisleys, very dark, almost black, and a striking Monet of sea, cliffs, distance, stillness. In the museum's coffee shop there is a view out of plate glass windows into an autumn garden: copper-coloured trees posing for Vlaminck.

Hobbling back to the flat I trip over a stone and my face is splat, smack, on the pavement. It's my right arm, however, that takes the brunt, grazed and gashed from wrist to elbow. I'm more shocked than hurt. There isn't much blood – not too many AIDS viruses are polluting this Netherlands street.

My arm is sore for days.

The conference, as far as I am concerned, has become a dead loss, so I decide to spend Saturday in Amsterdam. Trains in Holland are quick, frequent, cheap, clean, and they arrive and depart exactly when they are supposed to. I stare out at the Dutch countryside: because it is so level everything seems to happen in the distance, or at least that is where one's gaze is drawn; to the cluster of a town, a dark wood, a windmill etched on the sky. The foreground is like the marshlands of Somerset – fields separated by broad ditches (drains in Westcountry speech), pollarded willows and supine cows.

At Amsterdam Central I know something is wrong. My back has almost totally seized up: I can hardly move – it is worse than it has ever been. Why *now*? Some jolt of the train perhaps; I don't remember. Explanation brings no relief, nor do the anticipated pleasures of one of Europe's most beautiful cities. The warm autumn sunshine has given me a perfect day for simply pottering here, and, fuck! I won't be able to take advantage of it: what my senses register cannot dispel pain. So I note things dully, as if for future use in some inferior, drab place where the eye will need refreshment and the inner eye can do the work – the terraces of seventeenth-century houses, the October trees, the calm of so much still, silent water. The Oudekerk: amalgam, it seems, of everything good in every Dutch painting of an ecclesiastical interior; the high white walls, the certainties of the statement made by the glass, the attractive, unfussy bareness.

I abandon plans for the Rijksmuseum, the Van Gogh Museum. I'm too crippled.

But, for old times' sake, I must see the ancient heart of this city that grows out in layers of streets like an onion. All nights of all previous excursions to Amsterdam I shared John's bed in his flat in the Zeedijk – big, handsome Norwegian I met my first ever afternoon in Holland – and I remember, as I glance up at what were his windows, the song that was top of the charts when I was here in 1981, *Some people are made for each other ... some people can love one another for life; how about us?* It was not to be, and I don't know where he is now. He left Amsterdam for Copenhagen; I haven't heard from him in years. His kitchen, I recall, looked out on one of the canals, and I spent long moments just happily staring at the water. It seemed very romantic at the time: dancing at the D.O.K. ... candlelit dinners in Indonesian restaurants ... making love.

I go into a pornographic bookshop to buy a magazine which, if they found it in my luggage, would certainly arouse the interest of the Heathrow customs officers. I spend ages choosing (in fact I pause for a while to have tea and cakes in a nearby restaurant so I can mull over the selection); my eventual purchase is one of the most expensive. It isn't just the slim fit young bodies, the impressive cocks, the variety in the performances – two together, three together – sucking, fucking, licking, poking, prodding, pulling; nor even the excellent camerawork: it's because these particular young men seem to be hugely enjoying themselves. There is a real animal excitement, a rampant energy, in their gloriously upright erections thrusting into each other's hands and mouths and arseholes. All too often in these publications the actors look tired; the cocks aren't really stiff: it is joyless. A sham.

Its pages will adorn the walls of my bedroom and improve the quality of my wanking. For the nights at the D.O.K., the candlelit dinners, the love-making, are pleasures of the past. I remember from Latin lessons at school that the Romans could preface a question in three different ways – expecting the answer no (num), expecting the answer yes (nonne), and the third (ne) was if they

63

could not predict the answer. Do you want a grey-haired man of fifty-two who has the AIDS virus? There's no self-pity in that question, nor in the expected answer which is an inexorable fact of life – num.

Therefore my choice of magazine is important. It costs me thirty guilders.

My walk – crawl – to the station is one long hour of pain. I need a back transplant! A leg transplant! A whole new body! I feel derided, as Yeats said, by a sort of battered kettle at the heel:

> What shall I do with this absurdity –
> O heart, O troubled heart – this caricature,
> Decrepit age that has been tied to me
> As to a dog's tail?

The barrel organs roll out their music at the turnings of streets: exquisite nostalgia, these sound pictures of eras vanished long ago. Toys for children and adults that delight and hurt not. One of them – it thrills me to hear this – is playing the same tune Stravinsky listened to in, when was it? 1910, 1911? on a barrel organ in Paris; it became the most poignant theme of *Petrushka*. In the middle of the square outside the station a very good rock group is playing Bill Haley; a large appreciative audience is sitting in the road, thoroughly enjoying it. Only in Amsterdam … The station square in Rotterdam, I observe when I return, is empty. Tram-lines, leaves, bits of paper, dust. Dust, dust, dust.

I eat a pizza, then go to bed for an hour, having taken twice the number of pills for my back that I'm supposed to take. The result: I sleep the clock round, surfacing at nine a.m. on Sunday. I've missed the conference's last-night party and I had intended to be there.

But, thank God, my spine is not as bad as yesterday.

Looking for breakfast in Rotterdam on a Sunday morning is an utterly surreal experience. It is as if the Third World War had started and the city had been blitzed by neutron bombs – every building is intact; the traffic lights blink red, yellow, green, then green, yellow, red, but without point for the only cars and lorries are parked by the kerbs. There is apparently not one single human being left alive except myself. No cheerful Dutch families on bicycles, no kids taking the dog for a walk, no church-goers, no tourists, not even a solitary vagrant. It makes Dalston Junction at this hour look like the hub of the universe. Thoughts of breakfast recede, for there is no café or restaurant open. I'm starving. Eventually I find McDonald's — I never thought I would be grateful to find McDonald's in any city, but I am now. Until I read the menu: I cannot possibly eat this muck. I ask a waiter if there is anywhere else in Rotterdam serving breakfast. He deliberates at length with his colleagues who, like him, have nothing to do, for there are no customers. They all agree that there isn't.

But there is, and it's just across the street. I order coffee, a mushroom omelette, toast and marmalade, and eye up the chef, the only person in the restaurant apart from me. He's cute: tall, slim, dark hair and dark eyes, a little moustache. He's not wearing knickers under his tight trousers, and he's obviously pleased with the successful way the shape of his cock is outlined, for he notices what I'm looking at when he brings me the omelette, and smiles to himself. Deciding, presumably, that there will be no other patrons this morning, he goes out into the street and begins to wash his car. He leans against the rear window and scrubs the roof; I eat my omelette (delicious) and enjoy the curves of his arse, the swaying of his balls.

I find I am, more or less accidentally, by the cube houses that overlook the old harbour. They're as surreal as the whole of this morning has been — without doubt as odd as any houses anyone has ever built: cubes indeed, each balanced on one of its own edges so that they are diamond-shaped, and stuck on the tops of tall pillars — Simeon Stylites and his clones. Do *people* really live in them, I ask myself, or are they for travellers from outer space? One of them is a show house, and for a couple of guilders you can explore its inside. It is — remarkably for this city devoid of humans — open. The front door is at the foot of the pillar, and you climb a spiral staircase (the interior of the pillar) up to the house itself. Which is much

65

less cramped than I had imagined, with three storeys; the first contains the entrance hall, the kitchen, and a living room; the second a study, a bathroom, and a bedroom (humans obviously do live here despite its being a show house, for the enormous, comfortable bed has every sign of people having recently been in it); and the third has one room – another living room with a vast panorama of the sky. It is certainly O.K. for astronomers.

In fact I'm quite impressed by all this, except for the windows which, when they're not giving vistas of the sky, look straight into the other cubes. It would be like living in a tetrahedral goldfish bowl. I glimpse the various Sunday activitites of the cube-dwelling neighbours, a man reading a book, a woman drinking coffee, some children playing with cuddly toys. Only if you felt like giving an extremely public demonstration could you screw without shutting the curtains.

The girl at the desk in the entrance hall, when I ask how much it would cost to buy one of these places, says almost apologetically that they are very dear: about a hundred thousand guilders. Some quick arithmetic – less than thirty thousand pounds. *Unbelievably* cheap! Why on earth am I living in London?

In the afternoon I go to a sauna – good for my back, I tell myself – and find Rotterdam on a Sunday does have many human beings; gay male ones here, and naked, and on the hunt. Another man's hand bringing me to orgasm, I decide, is better than my own (even with the new porno mag to season it), and so, of course, it turns out to be. And the heat *is* good for my back.

I fly home with Tom, Paul Davies and Michael Carson. The customs men nod us through and therefore miss the three-fold pleasure of confiscating my magazine, persecuting a gay, and slobbering afterwards over the pictures. Tom is still on excellent form. We travel into town on the Piccadilly Line, and he notices someone reading a novel by J.G. Farrell. 'I knew Jim Farrell,' he says. 'He put me in that book! I must go and tell him!'

66

He gets up, and says to the novel-reader, 'I'm one of the characters in that book!' The man is interested, and asks, 'Which one?' 'Miriam,' Tom says. The man gives him a queer look, and jumps out of the train. (We are – luckily for him – at Leicester Square station.) When I've stopped laughing I say to Tom, 'Why do you think he got off?' Tom answers, 'Oh … doubtless to catch the Northern Line.'

Thinking about it all in the days that follow I conclude that it was a good week. More ups than downs. There are – it is certain – much worse weeks to come. This year? Next year? Some time? Look on the bright side … it may never happen … think of the books – *this* book – I still have to write.

All I know for sure is that it won't be never.

QUERCUS

Now that I am about to leave London for ever I have been asking myself what I shall be glad to abandon and what I shall miss. Music: it's unlikely that in Exmouth I'll find the same choice of concerts. I go to the Barbican or the Festival Hall two or three times a month, alone mostly since I lost my husband ten years back, though my friend Jemima – yes, that really is her name – occasionally comes with me. She's so choosy – an icky-picky Virgo – and she makes sweeping judgements of such grandeur I have to laugh. 'Oh, I don't listen to Prokofiev,' she said the other day, waving her hands about like windmills. Or: 'There's nothing really worthwhile in Sibelius, is there?' I rang her up to ask if she'd like to hear the Oriana Choir sing Mozart's *Requiem*. They were also doing the *Vesperae Solennes de Confessore* and the *Ave Verum Corpus*. Her answer left me speechless – one word: 'No.'

But we are both Shostakovich fans; we thoroughly enjoyed the recent season when they did all his orchestral music. We spent about fifty pounds each on that. I really shouldn't have done; I just don't possess that kind of money to splash out on luxuries. Or is it a luxury? My son Peter would say if I enjoy it so hugely it's a necessity. I have a good record player, but listening to canned music isn't the same as hearing it live – I can't concentrate so easily; it doesn't produce the same thrill; it doesn't move me. Jemima and I felt the best of the Shostakovich concerts was the fourth symphony and the first violin concerto (with Itzhak Perlman) at the Festival Hall. Ashkenazy conducted. That evening at the Barbican we could have heard *Pictures at an Exhibition* and

Oistrakh playing the Beethoven violin concerto. In what other city anywhere would you have to choose between Perlman and Oistrakh? Olivier Messiaen said he'd much rather spend his eightieth birthday in London than in Paris because we have the world's best music. He's right – we're spoiled.

I don't mind going on my own, particularly to the Barbican, which is much the better of the two concert halls acoustically and aesthetically. I get lost at the Festival Hall – the walkways outside don't seem to lead anywhere, and inside it's a maze, an architectural nightmare. No wonder Prince Charles said the whole South Bank complex looked like a vast incinerator. Why did they have to pull down the old Shot Tower? And what on earth is that ugly statue of Nelson Mandela doing? When I first noticed it – at a distance – I assumed it was one of our great composers, Elgar, Vaughan Williams, or Britten, but when I got close and saw who it really was I was very surprised. I've nothing against Nelson Mandela – I think it's a fearful crime that he's been locked away for a quarter of a century. But why put him *there*? I began to think that after all there was such a phenomenon as the lunatic left.

It disturbed me to think that. Because I can't say I'll be glad to bid goodbye to loony lefty boroughs and their politics – there aren't any. They're a figment of the fascist imagination. Our London councils do *not* make two-year-olds read filthy books or talk about person-hole covers, and they don't build cemeteries for lesbians. The only advantage I'll obtain from the Exmouth council is an efficient library service, which for an old woman of my age is important. The libraries in my London borough during the past three years have been closed more often than they've been open – it's a long-running dispute between the librarians and the council about staffing – but it isn't caused by the lunatic left; it's bloody-minded people being bloody-minded about other bloody-minded people. Both parties claim they want to give the rate-payers better value, but while they're working it out we get no value at all.

I'm leaving London because Peter has bullied me into it. He's been bullying me for years. What do you want that big old house for, Mum, rattling around in it all alone, one pea in a pod? What will you do if you're ill? I can't leave my work and nurse you; running a hotel is a full-time occupation. Why don't you sell up and live with Harry and me? (Harry is his lover.) We can look after you here; you'll have your own flat; you'll have company. No more solitary trips to concerts, solitary walks in the park, solitary evenings with the voices on the TV the only voices you listen to. That house is worth a fortune – why waste your one precious asset when you could be using it? You need that money and you need it now. Oh, of course I'd like inheriting it all, but that isn't the point. And so on and so on.

His arguments don't have any weight except the last. I *do* need the money. Otherwise … I'm in perfect health, mentally and physically; I like rattling around in my house, a small pea in a very big pod; I'm not at all sure I want to live with Peter and Harry, much as I love them; and I've learned to enjoy alone-ness. It was very hard when Douglas died but I think I made the correct decision – contrary to everyone else's advice, most of it unasked advice, which was to sell up. 'Make a fresh start,' they all said. At sixty! We'd lived in that house, Douglas and I, for thirty-two years; we'd grown into its fabric. It would be like having a limb chopped off. It *is* like having a limb chopped off. And I shall miss the garden. The hotel has a garden of course, but Peter employs a man who comes in and does it. Even if I took over the job it wouldn't be the same – it's not *my* garden. There are shrubs and trees here, herbaceous plants, we put in three decades back that are still going strong – some of them cut a little, others a mite tattered – but to me they are my children, adults now and drooping somewhat with the cares of the world, but nevertheless my children.

As for alone-ness – I enjoy being on my own. I don't traipse up to the Barbican to listen to old Jemima, but to hear what Johann Sebastian, Ludwig, Igor or Ben have to tell me. The same with my Sunday afternoon walks in Hyde Park. It amuses Peter that I go there every Sunday; why Sunday, Mum? Why not Tuesday? And why not a different park? There's Greenwich and St. James's and Richmond and a hundred others! I can't explain why it has to be Hyde Park – there isn't a reason. Just habit, I suppose, and the older you get the more you rely on habit. The young don't understand that, and I'm not so gaga I don't understand why they don't understand. The same thing will happen to them though they can't realise it now. Peter at forty-four is no longer young, bags of energy though he has; he's at that stage of life when he has his own routines and habits, but he's not yet aware he relies on them.

It's the trees I love in Hyde Park, the planes in particular. The plane is a grandfather of a tree: noble, majestic, beautiful at any time of the year. Its roots must dig very deeply indeed to tap water; why else does it require such little space in which to grow? You can surround it with concrete and it will continue to flourish. It even makes an oak look like a wimp, though I guess an oak lasts as long, is just as tough. I'm sure I haven't the majesty of a London plane, but I sometimes think I'm an oak – knotty, gritty, a bit dishevelled, but able to survive. Peter would laugh if I told him that. Quercus the oak.

Do I want to live with my son and his lover, gay proprietors of a gay hotel? I'll be surrounded by gays and I don't think I'll like it. I have nothing against them – and I mean that sincerely; I came to terms decades ago when Peter was nineteen. It's just that I'll be the one Gentile in a Jewish ghetto, the one Catholic in a Protestant church. The sort of alone-ness which isn't enjoyable. I might be wrong – I'll have to wait and see. When Peter told us he was gay I was sure of this point, and I made it very forcefully to Douglas, who was taking things harder than I was: 'If we don't accept it,' I said, 'we lose a child. Our only child.' Douglas soon agreed that there wasn't a choice. So we tried to be as supportive as we could and I think we did a reasonable job – we were there to console Peter when he was jilted by a lover and also there when he wanted us to meet a new lover. I became interested in the whole subject of homosexuality – not its causes; that seems irrelevant:

it simply *is* – but why, for example, people have always persecuted gays. At times I've become rather militant. Clause 28 made me furious, and I wrote to Dame Jill about it; 'Gays have families too,' I informed her. 'They all have mothers and fathers.' She didn't reply. I went on the march (I did not tell Jemima; she'd have thought I was off my head.) I waved a banner. I made it myself from an old sheet and I painted the words on it in pink: 'I love my gay son. Stop the persecution *now!*' I wanted it to be seen on television, so I deliberately stood behind Ian McKellen and the other famous people, thinking the cameras would be on them. Which they were. So there I was, on all four channels – for only about five seconds, but it was enough; millions could see that one grey-haired old soul who looks like everyone's idea of Grandma was prepared to stand up and be counted. Peter phoned and said it was embarrassing; he was watching the news with several gay friends at the time and he didn't know where to put himself. 'Who's in the closet?' I barked. 'You or me?' Then Harry came on and told me to take no notice; they were all tremendously proud. 'You would have been proud of *yourselves*,' I answered, 'if you'd closed that hotel for just one day and marched with me!'

Jemima didn't see the news, which was a good thing as I'd never have heard the end of it. (She'd gone to Sissinghurst with a bunch of her local O.A.P.s.)

The hardest part for us was when Peter took up with Harry. Peter, in his twenties, was a very male sort of man, a first-rate footballer and an even better tennis-player. Dressed to go out, his dark hair all sleeked down and his leather jacket on, he could look stunning. Douglas and I both thought he'd choose a younger man to live with, a … a softer man, more feminine than he was; that was the type he preferred though none of them lasted very long. Harry was quite a shock: years older, ugly – well, I thought he was ugly – and built like a brick wall. It was obvious to Douglas and me from the moment Harry appeared … What's the polite phrase they sometimes use? I can't remember. No, I have it: which way round they were. We didn't like to think of Peter being – not to put too fine a point on it – *penetrated*, though we said nothing of course. Not only that but he seemed to be happier with this one than with any of the waif-like kids he'd worshipped before. And he is still happy. Fifteen years they've been together and no end in sight; nor will there be now, I think – indeed I hope. For don't get me wrong: Harry is a wonderful man. I've grown to love him, my son-in-law, almost as much as I love Peter. It's simply that it wasn't easy to adjust to the … er … roles.

They've had the first floor of the hotel converted into a self-contained flat – the cost of this comes out of the sale of my house. It's very nice; my own kitchen, bathroom, bedroom, and my sitting room has a grandstand view of the sea. 'You'll *love* this view!' Peter said. 'Worth a million pounds it is!' I suppose he's right. In summer, yes: the light sparkling on the waves, the blue sky, the multi-coloured yachts tacking into the estuary, the distant shouts of children on the sand. And in the winter too it's exciting – storms and gales, huge breakers pounding the sea-wall, spray tossed high in the air, shingle flung onto the road.

> And he, the rebel, seeks the storm
> As if the storm could bring him peace.

Who said that? I can't remember. But for most of the year I'm afraid the view depresses me – in spring before the visitors arrive and in autumn when they've all gone it can be so forlorn; grey clouds, grey sea. Empty and grey. And the only sounds are the melancholy cries of gulls. I hate gulls. Cruel, primitive birds.

Peter will try to jolly me out of such moods. Think of the next concert, he'll tell me, and indeed there are concerts: the Bournemouth Symphony Orchestra plays in the Great Hall of Exeter University ten times a season, and I shall enjoy that, and going into the city with the other old-age pensioners on the coach that's hired especially for us. There's nothing wrong with the Bournemouth Symphony Orchestra but it won't be like London, choosing which concert, choosing which soloist, choosing which hall. There's no chance that in Exeter I'll have to decide between Perlman and Oistrakh. I shouldn't think either of them has *heard* of Exeter. Or Peter will say, 'Come downstairs and eat with us. You don't have to be miserable up here by yourself.' He'll open a bottle of wine, and Harry will have some amusing stories to tell – he's a great raconteur – and we'll play cards, and talk about politics or trips abroad or the hotel business or even sex; I'll enjoy myself ... but in some little part of my brain I'll be thinking I'd be happier on my own watching *Newsnight* or reading a good book in bed.

Peter can't understand my attachment to London. When he and Harry bought the hotel he said they were both delighted to leave the capital and not for one moment have they had a single regret. The crime in the streets, the litter – 'It's the filthiest city in the world, Mum' – and the problems with traffic; the time involved in even the shortest of journeys; the tension it creates. What else, I asked. Oh ... things that wouldn't bother you, Mum – the gay bars and discos where you don't know a soul and no one will speak unless you're twenty and extremely cute. Isn't that the same everywhere, I asked. Not at all, he said. There's just one pub he's been to in Devon, and if he and Harry drink in there on a Friday night (which they don't very often; weekends they are busy at the hotel, summer and winter) they know most of the people. 'That doesn't happen in London,' he said. He pushed a newspaper at me: 'And down here I don't have to read this sort of nonsense.' It was one of the free papers they have in gay pubs; a couple who'd gone that morning had left it behind in their room. I glanced through it. Well ... I could see what Peter meant.

I'm supposed to go to the solicitor's tomorrow and sign the contract on the sale. I'm still not sure. I could ring Jemima, but she'll be no help. 'Either you sign it or you don't sign it,' she'll say. 'Those are your choices.' I need the money: I can't afford to pay the rates this year if I don't sell, let alone think about a holiday or a new hat or the Concertgebouw next month at the Barbican. (It's Haitink; Mozart's *Jupiter* and Schubert's *Great C Major*, and the ticket will cost me, if I want a good seat, which

I do, seventeen pounds.) And the house needs a fortune spent on it – I really should have central heating put in; there's a gutter to be replaced; some of the bathroom floorboards are soft; the kitchen wall bulges; I'm worried about security (I ought to get a burglar alarm); and it all needs redecorating from top to bottom, inside and out. My pension and my savings just won't cope with that *and* keeping me alive as well.

I'm going to break my rule and walk in Hyde Park even though it's Monday. I'll stare at the plane trees and have a good long think: there are times when I know I'm not quercus the oak at all.

I didn't recognize the man who came up to me by the Serpentine, but when he told me who he was I could see who he had been twenty years ago – Keith, a management trainee of some sort then, now a financial adviser to a property company. An ex-lover of Peter's. I looked at the mature man, lined and a bit thin on top, but I saw the youth I remembered. We had tea in the café by the lake and we talked for an hour: and perhaps because we were almost strangers we spoke of the problems on our minds. His lover of the past seven years has AIDS; is in hospital, a living skeleton, demented, beyond hope – so whether or not I should sign the contract sitting on my lawyer's desk seemed a trivial matter. 'Don't do it,' he said. 'It would be an awful mistake.'

'Why?'

'Peter will drown you with kindness. Killing you softly with his song. That's why I left him.'

We stared at each other. He was, of course, absolutely right.

We returned to the subject of his dying lover, with whom he had thought, he said, to spend all the rest of his life. Thirty years. We exchanged phone numbers and promised to keep in touch.

I walked back to Marble Arch and as I looked up at the plane trees I scarcely noticed them. Why should there be AIDS? What is the point, the purpose of cutting young men down in their prime? It is all so meaningless. Life itself is so meaningless. Why should the desires and hopes and energies of youth wither away? Why should disappointment be so frequent in our lives? If some terrible disease, a car crash, a war, doesn't kill us prematurely, we become dull and uninteresting before we've started to live. We eat and drink and have sex and we die; we spawn others to take our places, and they're just as stupid and silly as we are. Even at school pettiness and lack of imagination destroy what little originality we bring into this world. We fill London with hideous buildings and poison it with exhaust fumes and dash about all over it to no real end; we pursue illusions or bodies or money or status and at seventy we look back and see that we've influenced nothing, altered nothing, done nothing. We complain of depression and swallow drugs or paralyse ourselves with booze; we ignore our past and hope the present will go as quickly as possible because tomorrow perhaps will be better; but it's all a game, an idiotic charade we indulge in to prevent ourselves seeing truths so awful we'd have no alternative but to jump in front of the next passing bus. Why are lovers so selfish, so unkind? They swear to be generous and sensitive and faithful unto death; they talk of fulfilment, of joy, of ecstasy, but they lie and cheat; they weigh up what they can get out of each other and give nothing in return, use and abuse one another until feeling is murdered and they're off to claw and seize and defile the next corpse. Why is there no God?

I leaned against a tree – an oak – and started to cry.

Where do these dark thoughts come from? Everyone isn't like that. Peter and Harry aren't like that. Nor, I would guess, are Keith and his lover. Douglas and I certainly weren't. So why this knowledge? This need to atone? This emptiness? This ... despair?

I've decided not to sell. The decorating is of little importance – the paper can peel off the walls; it doesn't matter – and I can heat the rooms with a paraffin stove. The gutter can fall down, the bathroom rot, the kitchen bulge till it bursts open. I shall stay here with the flowers and trees we planted in 1957; I shall go to my concerts (I've already phoned the Barbican and booked for the Concertgebouw) and I shall continue to walk on Sundays in Hyde Park. I rang Jemima and told her; she said I was being foolish and hasty – 'You always were, dear.' I didn't ask if she wanted to come with me to the Concertgebouw.

I shall have to ring Peter. He won't understand; he'll be disappointed and annoyed. He may even create a scene, or send Harry up to London to talk me out of it. I think I'll phone Keith as well; he'd be amused. And I want to know how his lover is tonight.

I was just about to dial Peter – it took a large sherry to give me the courage – when the phone rang. Keith. His lover is no worse, but it's merely a question of time. Days, not weeks. I told him of my decision, and he asked whether his remark about Peter killing me softly with his song had influenced me.

'Yes,' I said.

'I … I might be able to help you.'

'In what way?'

'Have you ever thought that your bank or a property company might be interested in buying your house? Below the market value … but it's possible you could go on living there and you'd have the money they paid. It depends on all sorts of things … the state of the house, how long they'd expect you to live … I can't promise … I could be raising false hopes, but it's worth thinking about.'

I have made an appointment to see him at nine a.m. tomorrow morning.

THE MERCHANT'S TALE

The preliminaries – the kissing, the slow removal of each other's clothes, the naked embraces on the bed, the exploration of skin by fingers, the sucking of nipples, the hands at last grabbing balls and manipulating cocks – were done; and they were now, though nowhere close to a grand finale, at a very pleasant second stage: the sixty-nine position – mouths sucking cocks, tongues licking balls, pubic hair, arseholes. They had done this many times, so they knew each other's geography well enough to tread more quickly – or more slowly – on ground that elicited sensations of maximum pleasure. There were frequent pauses for the inhaling of poppers. Then the phone rang.

'Who the fuck can that be?' Michael asked. (It was his hotel room.) 'This is Florence! Nobody knows I'm here.'

'Dennis does,' Rick said. Dennis was Rick's one-to-one, live-in lover of seven years' standing.

'In that case I'm certainly not answering it!'

'I'm curious to know what he wants. Why he's calling now.'

'Well … ' Michael picked up the receiver. 'Hullo,' he said. 'Michael Robinson.' As if he were in England.

It *was* Dennis. 'Michael! We've both been in this city for three days and we haven't met! I'd thought our paths would cross at the Uffizi or the Accademia; somewhere … What have you been doing? What are you doing now? Why don't you come out and have a drink with me?'

'Me? Not *us*? Isn't Rick with you?' Michael looked at Rick, whose blond head was so efficiently at work on his cock that he was afraid he might gasp or cry out. Rick's hands were also groping his balls in a particularly rough and pleasurable way.

'I haven't seen Rick for hours,' Dennis said. 'I suppose he's enjoying a bit of the night-life.'

'Doesn't that worry you? He could be having his arse screwed off by some hunky Julio or massive Giuseppe.'

'Rick doesn't do that sort of thing! We trust each other completely in that department ... He's bopping somewhere. He likes disco dancing and I don't. Question of age ... I'm thirty-nine, and he's ten years younger.'

'I'm thirty-nine and I like slogging it out on the disco floor.'

'Come and have a drink. There's a nice little bar in the Via dei Castellani, near the Ponte Vecchio.'

'It's late,' Michael said. 'And I'm tired. Eleven thirty ... I'm in bed.'

'Alone?'

'Yes. I'm reading a book ... Benvenuto Cellini's *Memoirs*.'

Rick, needing to laugh silently, stopped sucking, which was just as well as Michael, to his own surprise, was so turned on by the situation – Rick sucking his cock while he talked to Dennis – that instead of being embarrassed or alarmed he feared he might come immediately. He shifted his position, lying now on his back and leaning against the wall. Rick opened the KY tube and began to massage both cocks with what he liked to call the juice of life, and even more exquisite sensations were produced. Michael had to restrain him with his free hand.

'Benvenuto Cellini,' Dennis said. 'How very appropriate ... his statue is on the Ponte Vecchio. Have you been to the Uffizi yet?'

'I was there this morning.'

'So were Rick and I! I wonder how we didn't see you ... Isn't it superb? You just turn a corner and there on the wall is Uccello's *Rout of San Romano*. There's a daft story I heard about Uccello the other day. He was busy one evening, painting away in his studio, when Mrs Uccello shrieked up to him, "Paolo! Your dinner's ready! It's on the table!" "I won't be five minutes," he yelled back. Five minutes became half an hour, an hour, and Paolo's spaghetti was congealed and frozen. When Mrs U. had finished eating, she went upstairs to see what the matter was, thus becoming the first person ever to experience *The Rout of San Romano*. "I've discovered perspective!" Paolo cried, and fell to the floor in a dead faint.'

'I don't believe a word of that!' Michael said. 'Though I suppose he did discover perspective. It's the lances, isn't it? The knights on horseback waving those spears – it makes them seem as if they're one behind another.'

'A moot point, I would think. There's perspective of a sort in Fra Angelico, and if I remember rightly – I'm not certain – he pre-dates Uccello.'

'They were born in the same year.'

'Oh. Have you been to the convent of St. Mark?'

'Not yet.'

'Absolutely packed, my dear, with Fra Angelicos! Including the famous *Annunciation*. Every cell in that convent has a Fra Angelico on the wall. Very pretty colours, reds and blues and golds so vivid they look as if they were done last week, but all a bit depressing. You know ... the medieval world, doom and gloom, nothing worthwhile in human life, the emphasis always on the goodies in Heaven afterwards. They hated the body, I think. The B.V.M.'s reaction in *The Annunciation* to the news that she's going to have a child ... she seems to be suffering from a nasty bout of diarrhoea. And Fra Angelico can't make Heaven interesting ... all simpering angels, haloes, clouds and harps ... Everyone looks so bored! The Hell bits are more exciting. There's even a great hairy devil in one fresco, horns and forked tail and so on, and he's buggering a man. Probably a *gigantic* plonker. So Hell can't be too bad, I say, though Fra Angelico certainly doesn't give the impression that he approves of it – the buggery, I mean.'

Rick had stopped his massage. He leaned over the side of the bed and took a condom out of his shirt pocket. He held it up, questioningly: Michael nodded. Rick tore off the cellophane, and slowly unrolled the contents onto Michael's erection. They both wanted to giggle – it was bright blue. He took a vast sniff of poppers, then put them under Michael's nose; he too sniffed long and deep. Rick was now straddling Michael, a thigh on either side of the torso, and he lowered himself onto the cock, which slid easily and gently into his arse. He began to move up and down, stretching forward so that his tongue could lick eyelids and ears, his teeth bite ear-lobes. His hands twisted nipples.

When Michael spoke, the effect of the amyl was such that his voice seemed to him to be coming from the bottom of a well. 'You're right,' he said to Dennis. 'Medieval man was hedged in by every conceivable Thou Shalt Not. The only surprise is that the Middle Ages continued for so long ... illustrates the awful power of the Church, the dead hand of Roman Catholicism. In the Uffizi you go from *The Rout of San Romano* into the next room, and there, suddenly, like a blinding revelation, are all the most famous Botticellis. It's as if you're seeing the inception of modern man. The Renaissance begins *here*! You could even say the twentieth century begins here ... *The Birth of Venus*, *The Madonna of the Pomegranate*, the *Primavera*. Botticelli's the first post-medieval painter to discover the marvel of the human body. There's a *revelling* in it ... joy, release ... excitement at our potential to live, to be happy. They're the only paintings I've ever seen that have moved me to tears, as they did when I last saw them, decades ago – I was nineteen. Those paintings *dance*. They tell us we're free; we can be fulfilled, love, think for ourselves!'

'I doubt Botticelli was the first to know all that. He wasn't alone. He could do what he did because he's reflecting the current feeling and thought of his age. His civilization. What it was like to be in Florence then. Petrarch, Boccaccio, Dante, Machiavelli, Galileo, Michelanglo, Leonardo da Vinci, Donatello and so on were Florentines too.'

'But not at the same time. Petrarch and Boccaccio were well before.'

'Some were his contemporaries, or around soon after. And Botticelli isn't always happy ... the faces in *The Madonna of the Pomegranate*, even the children, are certainly beautiful, but they're fearfully sad.'

'Yes, I noticed that and I wondered why.'

'Have you noticed that the faces and bodies of young people you see in the streets here often look remarkably like those in Botticelli?'

'Yes. As if a gene has been passed on, and is still working hard.' The face nuzzled against his, the cock, slippery with KY, he was handling, the body he was fucking, had, despite the curly blond hair and blue irises of a more northern latitude, something of a Botticelli youth: the vigour and the fact that he too was celebrating the greatest pleasure of being alive. There might not be much of Florence's Renaissance intellect in what Rick was doing, but there was an echo of its spirit. And the labyrinthine betrayals of its history.

'Florence gives us back our faith in the body,' Dennis declared. '*The Birth of Venus* is truly astonishing! This lovely young woman, shy in her nakedness; an attendant on her left rushing to cover her with a gorgeous cloak, while on the other side the two figures that are flying – the zephyrs – are blowing so fiercely that there's no possibility she'll get that cloak on ... Yes, you're right; it *is* the beginning of modern man. And, yes, it does dance. You know, even Lippo Lippi paints virgins with beautiful faces. *If* they were virgins! So young ... they can't be more than about fourteen or fifteen. Incredible! All those artists were caught up in the prevailing zeitgeist.'

'The prevailing what?'

'Zeitgeist. The Venetians never were; their history is so different ... They were concerned with making money and ripping off the Byzantines and stealing other people's statues and saints' bones. The bronze horses on St Mark's were nicked from the Emperor in the Fourth Crusade. I know they had their great painters, Veronese, Titian, Tintoretto, the Bellinis, Canaletto, Guardi and so on, but did one of them ever paint an attractive human body? They didn't. Yes, you see nude men and women wriggling in and out of coy remnants of flying drapery, but none of them is done with any loving care. None! Two exceptions ... a *Lazarus* by one of the Bassanos, and a dead Christ by Messina. Now they do look like real naked flesh and skin, but Messina wasn't a Venetian – he just happened to be passing through at the time and he was asked to knock off a dead Christ. Probably to pay his hotel bill.'

'There's something about this place,' Michael said, 'that's peculiarly vibrant ... the countryside, the mountains ... Florence set in a bowl. Yesterday I climbed up to San Miniato. Elegant, peaceful church, and the views are *stunning*! The whole city at one's feet. The same from the Boboli Gardens, or Fort Belvedere. And this weather for March ... superb!'

'It isn't always March. And the Boboli Gardens are boring. So are most of the palaces – stuffy, grandiose, tasteless. And the cathedral's a dull elephant.'

'Inside, I grant you. But the exterior is delicious, like coconut ice ... you could eat it. And don't forget the baptistery doors. Those bronze carvings! Did you know Florence wept for joy at the end of World War Two when they were replaced? I can quite understand why.'

Rick, feeling that this discussion of art and history was beginning to cause a lessening of the intensity in Michael's hand, put his own hands on his cock. Michael took the hint. He anointed the cock with more KY and increased the friction. This, and an application of poppers, restored Rick to the level of bliss that he wanted, and he nearly gasped.

'Florence is very rowdy,' Dennis went on. 'The narrow streets funnel and amplify noise ... the noise of cars in particular, and those absurd pop-pop machines Italians will ride on. They drive like maniacs, and if you dare venture onto a zebra crossing, they deliberately try to run you over! I haven't slept well since I've been here; I'm continually being disturbed in the small hours by gangs of youths yelling in the street below. Yes, *gangs* of them! It's the school journey season ... should be prohibited by law. What on earth do these kids get out of the museums and churches of Florence? Almost nothing, I should think; they're far too young to appreciate Brunelleschi and Giotto. I'm not surprised they behave so badly! It's all an excuse for impoverished teachers to fiddle a free holiday, in my opinion ... These kids run amok in the

Uffizi and elsewhere, and ruin other people's enjoyment. I could hardly get near the *Primavera* for guides explaining it in six different languages to six different parties of adolescents, none of whom were the least interested. How can you enjoy one of the world's greatest paintings with that racket going on? You can't. I had to return later when they'd moved elsewhere, hoping and praying I wouldn't get caught up in some other miserable crocodile of acned teenagers. Do you know, in St. Mark's convent, there was an American lecturing a group of extremely bored eight-year-olds on the finer points of Fra Angelico? *Eight*-year-olds! It's utterly ludicrous.'

'Oh, I agree. I agree. But Florence, unlike London, has almost no litter on the pavements; the Arno has fish in it; I love the church bells, and the food in the restaurants is cheap and awfully well cooked. And Santa Croce and San Lorenzo and the Medici chapel, which is surely the world's most dignified, pomp-and-circumstance funeral parlour, with Michelangelo statues thrown in – even if his women are really men with big tits and no cocks. It's easy to see why E.M. Forster adored Florence, prissy old aunt that he was: a taste of freedom. A room that undoubtedly has a view.'

There was a pause; Michael concentrated on thrusting deeply into Rick. It wouldn't be long, he felt, before he had to come – the expression on Rick's face and the trembling in his limbs showed he was also very near.

'What else have you been doing?' Dennis asked.

'I went to a concert. Rachmaninov's *Paganini Variations* and the Shostakovich eighth.'

'Shostakovich, Shostakovich! He gets in everywhere these days! I sometimes think he's performed more often than Beethoven, Mozart or Tchaikovsky. Why?'

'Since glasnost Russia is the flavour of the month. The flavour of the decade. There's more news on the TV about Russia than there is about America. And almost every week there's a programme on Russian ballet dancers, or Westerners travelling to Irkutsk or Estonians in folk costume singing their heads off. Anyway ... what's wrong with Shostakovich?'

'Nothing. The eighth is very fine. A bit lengthy perhaps; you keep thinking the last movement's about to stop, then it starts again. The fourth's his best.'

'No. The fifteenth.'

Another silence, which Michael took advantage of to get at the poppers. He had reached the point where two or three really good shoves would produce sperm, but if he held back he could last just a little longer. The pleasure was already acute: orgasm, he knew, was going to be tremendous. The same, it would appear, for Rick. He wasn't now manipulating Rick's cock, merely holding his free hand round it so Rick could control his plunges – pause, thrust slowly; pause, thrust slowly.

'Have you seen the Michelangelos in the Accademia?' Dennis asked.

'The statues for Julius the Second's tomb are quite amazing! Like men imprisoned in stone! There's one figure who seems to be heaving mightily, trying to push the marble off his face so he can breathe. So he can be born. They're like huge embryos pleading for life.'

'And the *David*?'

'Odd. It only seems to work when you're some distance from it. Close to, everything's out of proportion. The thighs are a bit stubby, the right hand is too big and the right arm's much too long; no one's arms could reach that far down their leg. But the genitalia are gorgeous! I could *eat* them! I think it's the one part of the body that he sculpted with the most care and attention. The little wrinkles in the foreskin, the hole at the tip, the balls ... he *knew* those balls! Only someone who'd used them often – and well – could carve them so accurately.'

Without realising what he was doing, Michael illustrated his point by giving Rick's balls an extra hard twist. Rick groaned.

'What was that?' Dennis asked.

'What was what?'

'I distinctly heard someone groan. As if he was about to come.'

'Nonsense!'

'I *heard* him! You can't fool me!'

85

'Well … as you require the intimate details … I'm having a wank.'

'It didn't sound like you.'

'How do you know what I sound like when I'm having a wank?'

'The same as everyone else I imagine. I meant it seemed … further off. *Is* there a man in your bed?'

'If you really must know … yes.'

'Who?'

'An Italian youth I picked up in the Boboli Gardens,' Michael said. 'He's called Lorenzo.'

'The Magnificent, no doubt. And you've been talking to me all this time! How remarkably bizarre!'

'It's turned us both on.'

'It's turning me on as well. Does he speak English?'

'Scarcely a word. Why?'

'I suppose I may as well have some fun as Rick is dancing his tits off God knows where: describe him to me. Is he good in bed?'

'You want this to become a pornographic phone-in? A sort of gay-line? When we were discussing high-minded things like Renaissance Art! Well … he's almost perfect in bed. And he's blond … unusual for an Italian. Blond in the pubes, too. Lovely muscly thighs, with a light scattering of golden hairs. Smooth chest. Good curve to the biceps. Big, dangling balls, the type you can't stop groping. And a very respectable uncircumcised cock, seven or eight inches and quite thick. Firm as a telegraph pole. And if you really want the cinema vérité, I'm pounding my piledriver of a fuckstick up his juicy arse. Aided and abetted by a blue condom, which is about to be filled with *wads* of sperm.'

Dennis roared with laughter. 'Pile-driver of a fuckstick! Wads of sperm! What language! I prefer you on the subject of Botticelli or E.M. Forster. It's strange … you could have been describing Rick.'

'Really? How very interesting! I wouldn't mind … one of these days … getting my hands into Rick's bloomers.'

'Not a chance. Not a chance in the world! He's the most faithful of men. I trust him totally.'

Rick signalled that he was about to come. 'Do you want to hear Lorenzo's orgasm?' Michael asked. 'It's ... on its way!'

'Sure. Why not?'

He held out the receiver so that it was an inch or two from Rick's mouth, and Rick erupted: shuddered, gasped, cried out; sperm shot up onto his chest, into Michael's hair, into the earpiece of the phone. Sweating, panting, he collapsed in Michael's arms.

'Pretty good,' Michael said.

'Sounded like an earthquake. It's given me an erection ten miles high.'

'I'm shifting him onto his back so I can get a better fucking position. Then you can hear me too.'

'I'm sure you'll sound a little more discreet, my dearest, but you needn't bother. Rick's just blown in, somewhat earlier than I expected ... so I'm going to pound *my* piledriver up *his* arse. Goodnight.' He rang off.

They said nothing for a while so Michael could enjoy coming, and, though his orgasm was as colossal as he'd felt it would be, the noise of it was indeed less of an earthquake than Rick's.

'What did he mean,' Michael said at last, 'that you had just blown in? It's all too ... weird!'

'Fantasy,' Rick answered. 'Wish fulfilment.' He unpeeled the blue condom and inspected what was in it.

'I think he's perfectly well aware it was *your* orgasm he heard. You overdid it a bit, didn't you? I mean, it was ... *loud*! He knows we're having it off behind his back ... He's playing some game with us, maybe a dangerous game. Dangerous for *us*. The laugh isn't on him, ultimately.'

'I didn't overdo it. It was one of the most terrrific orgasms I've ever had! I'm still ... *shaking*! God! You're marvellous! And Dennis has no idea. I'm certain of that; he was telling the truth when he said he trusts me. For a man in his fortieth year, he's incredibly naive.'

'What we did was ... very unkind.'

'Not at all. If he hasn't the slightest suspicion, how can it be unkind?'

'Because,' Michael said, 'an act is good or bad in itself; not merely good or bad according to its consequences. I feel ... ashamed.'

'I don't.' Rick started to play with Michael's balls again. 'It was ... *ecstasy*! And no harm has been done. Don't be philosophical; fucking isn't a subject to be philosophical about.'

'Why not?'

'You're simply meant to enjoy it.'

'Why don't you leave him?'

Rick stared. 'Oh, no,' he said. 'I'd never do that. Never! He's my soul-mate!'

'And what am I?'

'Excitement.'

'And there's no excitement with him?'

'Not sexually. We've been together so long. It's very nice ... comfortable and soothing. But ... predictable. Don't look so forlorn! You and I are superb in the sack; a bitter fit than Dennis and I were even at our peak. And you have a *great* body; I can't get enough of it! Black as soot all over ...'

'Excitement.'

'Yes! With you ... all my fantasies have a chance of being realised.'

'What kind of fantasies?'

'I'm not sure anything could be as perfect as just now, Dennis hearing my orgasm and not having a clue it was me. But ... I want ... to do it covered in oil. I mean, immersed in a *drum* of oil. Or in risky public places ... a park or a beach, or a cubicle of a toilet. I want you literally to *tear* my clothes off! Do it with a third person. Or four, or five. Have videos made of it. I want two cocks up my arse at the same time. I want you to handcuff me to the bed and beat the shit out of me with a leather strap!'

'It could all be arranged, I suppose.'

'I knew you'd say yes. Dennis *never* would.'

'The drum of oil is a bit of a tall order. But not impossible. As for thrashing your arse ... that appeals! Tingling buttocks ...'

'The whole programme has given us both very stiff erections. Shall we ... make use of them?'

'Of course.'

'Can I fuck you? Then suck you off.' He leaned over the bed and took another condom out of his pocket, and fitted it on himself. It was green. 'Environmental,' he explained. 'Ozone friendly.'

'The greatest excitement I can think of,' Michael said as Rick's cock eased itself into his arsehole, 'would be to do it without condoms. We'd have to have an AIDS test first, both of us ... and if we're negative, then ... '

'That can be arranged too. Christ! The next few months are going to be *sensational*!'

And after that, Michael said to himself, over and over as they clawed and clutched, and their cocks lunged and their tongues plunged, as they sweated and whimpered and moaned, what then? What then? We'll soon be bored. And begin again the hunt for other cocks to impale and poke our flesh, other orifices to grope and scrape. It's so utterly futile. Not like Botticelli at all.

ADAM, TAP AND THE DRAGON

For Adam, on his fifth birthday

Once upon a time there was a boy called Adam. He had grey-blue eyes and long, long eyelashes. His hair was neat and straight and he had beautiful white teeth. He lived in a thatched cottage on the edge of a forest.

One day he went for a walk in the forest all by himself. He had never been alone in the forest before. 'Take care of yourself,' said his mother, and she gave him twenty pence and some chewing-gum because he liked chewing gum. So off he went into the forest.

He had not gone very far when he heard a most awful TERRIFYING roar. He could hardly believe his ears. Or eyes: there, in front of him, on the ground in a clearing between the trees was a huge, gigantic, enormous, green DWAGON.

'If I stand very still and pretend I'm not here,' Adam said to himself, 'perhaps he will not see me and go away.' So he pretended very hard, and though the DWAGON roared even more loudly Adam found that he wasn't there, just as he had wanted; and he found he was somewhere else, in another part of the forest instead.

'What's the matter with you?' said a voice at his elbow. Adam looked down and saw a funny little old man with a long white beard.

'I'm lost,' Adam said.

'Where do you want to go?' the old man asked.

'I don't know,' Adam replied.

'I can't tell you where to go,' said the old man, 'if you don't know where you want to go.'

'What's your name?' Adam asked.

'Tap,' said the old man. 'What's yours?'

'Adam,' said Adam. 'Where do you live?'

'In a drain, ' said Tap, 'with my friends Fox-Box, Tra-la-la and Tree.'

'I don't like drains,' said Adam.

'They're very comfortable,' said Tap. 'Warm in winter, because everyone has hot baths, and cool in summer, because everyone has cold showers.'

'Oh,' said Adam.

At that moment there was a terrible HORRIBLE roar, and the DWAGON appeared.

'Don't mind him,' said Tap. 'His bark is worse than his bite. He's hungry.'

'Will he eat me?' Adam asked.

'He would rather have a bucket full of coal,' said Tap, and he dived head-first into the drain, and came back with a bucket full of coal. The DWAGON ate it all up. Then he lay down to sleep, purring loudly because he was pleased. A few long tongues of flame came out of his mouth when he snored.

'Very useful creatures, DWAGONS,' said Tap. 'When my drain gets too wet, which it does sometimes when too many children use too much water in their baths, he comes inside and dries it for me.'

'What's his name?' Adam asked.

'Holly,' said Tap.

'Oh,' said Adam.

'Don't you have a DWAGON in your house?' Tap asked.

'No,' said Adam.

'That's strange,' said Tap. 'What happens when your house gets all wet inside?'

'It doesn't get wet inside very often,' Adam said. 'Once the lavatory overflowed because my brother threw too much paper into it, and my dad was cross because he had to unblock the drain. The DWAGON would have been very useful then.'

'Next time that happens,' said Tap, 'I'll lend you my DWAGON.'

'Thank you very much,' said Adam. 'Though I don't

know what my mum would say if a DWAGON came into her house.'

'Why?' Tap asked.

'Its flames might burn the carpets and the curtains,' Adam said.

'If you lived in a drain,' said Tap, 'you wouldn't have to worry about things like that.'

'True,' said Adam.

'Would you like a ride on the dragon?' Tap asked.

'I thought it was called a DWAGON,' Adam said.

'Dragon or DWAGON, it's all the same,' Tap said. 'Do you want a ride or don't you?'

Adam did not know what to say. He wanted to ride on the dragon's back more than anything else in the whole world. Well, who wouldn't? But he was afraid of the dragon's mouth. He might get burned.

'Yes, please,' he said at last, plucking up courage.

'It will cost you twenty pence,' said Tap.

'All right,' said Adam, and he gave Tap the twenty pence Mum had given him. It's not every day, he said to himself, that I have a chance to ride on a dragon. Let alone a DWAGON. It looked safe at the moment, fast asleep, its tail curled round its body and its neck. But it *was* very large. And very fiery. Still, his brother had never ridden a dragon. What a story he would be able to tell him!

'Wake up!' Tap shouted at the dragon. The dragon opened one eye. 'Take this boy for a ride!'

Adam climbed onto the dragon's back, and in no time at all they were flying high over the forest. It was marvellous. The dragon took good care not to breathe out flames and smoke, so Adam really enjoyed himself.

'Thank you very much,' said Adam, when they landed in Adam's back garden. 'Help yourself to some coal.' The dragon, pleased, did so, for it was parked right outside the coal-shed.

'Did you have a nice time?' Adam's mother asked when he went indoors.

'I had a ride on a DWAGON,' said Adam.

'What fibs you do tell!' said his mother.

'I did! He's outside now, eating coal!'

They went into the garden to have a look. But the dragon had gone. And Adam never saw him again.

ON NARBERTH MOUNTAIN

I have literally hundreds of distant cousins – twice removed, three times removed – in Little England Beyond Wales. Almost no Reeses have left South Pembrokeshire in the past two centuries, my grandfather being an exception. It is not hard to see why. The indigenous Welsh were driven out by marauding Vikings and into the vacant space flowed waves of colonists – English, Norse, Flemish and Irish – and their descendants to this day have regarded their territory as an island, surrounded on three sides by the sea and on the fourth by hostile Welsh-speaking Celts with whom they have little contact. The Normans built a chain of castles stretching from Laugharne to Roche to keep the Welsh at bay, and so successful was this device that even now the people south of these castles speak English, to the north Welsh. This language frontier is called the Landsker. North Pembrokeshire is mountainous; the farming poor; it is dominated by chapels. In the south the churches are English in style; the land is good; the climate warmer, not unlike that of Devon and Cornwall. My relatives have stayed where they are because living standards are better and they don't speak Welsh. But to me, an outsider, they seem very Welsh – their accents, their appearance, their lack of reserve, their interests in singing and rugby – though *their* feelings about Welshness are full of contradictions. 'If Wales became independent as the Nationalists want,' my cousin Wyndham said, 'we wouldn't stand for it! There would be a civil war, like in Ulster!' But mainly their grumbles are about television programmes in Welsh; and 'Oh, she's from the Welsh!' they say in derogatory tones of some North Pembrokeshire girl

94

who has married into our family, as if it explained every-thing about her that is wrong. Yet they feel no allegiance to England. 'I'm a Welshman and I'm proud of it!' I heard Arthur Rees – my great-grandfather's brother's grandson – say in a pub to an English tourist. A few days previously he had been complaining about an acquaintance whose faults, he said, were typical of a Welsh-speaking Welshman. This ambivalence sits on them easily. Their horizons are the edges of South Pembrokeshire and always have been.

The polyglot origins can be heard in the Babel of place names, and what magnificent names they are – Stackpole Elidor, Elegug Stacks, Skokholm, Uzmaston and Gumfreston, Cosheston and Bosherston, Stepaside, Red Roses, New Hedges, Martletwy, Tavernspite, Landshipping, Angle, Crunwere, Skrinkle, Warren and Wooden. You have to cross the Landsker to find Welsh names – Henllan Amgoed and Maenclochog. And so it is with the names of my relatives: their polyglot ori-gins, too, roll off the tongue like defiant statements; challenges to that other tribe on the far side of the castles – Dora Chedzoy, Cissie Skyrme, Lilian Noot, Rosanna Brawn, Florence Furlong, Florence Louvain Calver, Bartlett Shanklin Rees, Eunice Ann Scourfield, Vivian Laura Firks, Simon Smith-Wrench, Lawford William Lyndon Merriman, Daisy Alexandra Rees Gwyther.

Our common ancestor was Bartlett Rees, who was born at Ludchurch in 1795, son of Benjamin and Maria Rees (née David). On the fifth of December 1818 he married Ann Hooper, whose occupation in the census returns is given as 'she toiled in the fields.' They both died in Narberth Workhouse, he in 1863, she in 1874. He was an agricultural labourer at Molleston Back, a farm on the slopes of Narberth Mountain. (Mountain is an absurd misnomer; it's an unremarkable small hill.) The cottage they lived in, and in which both my great-grandfather and my grandfather were born, is so tiny no humans would live in it now: it is Molleston Back's cowshed. I have frequently wondered about this odd Christian name, Bartlett. For it is my middle name and that of both my brothers, my nephew Peter, my father and his brother, my grandfather and my great-grandfather. Some of the distant cousins have it too, not only Bartlett Shanklin Rees, but also Bartlett John Rees, John Bartlett Morris and Stanley Bartlett Ronald Rees. It is not the surname of a woman who married into the family – but it is so unusual, and so many of us have it, that it must be of significance. Nobody knows what that significance is; none of the cousins has any explanation. It's lost, a signpost pointing to a place that has disappeared, a rune in the indecipherable alphabet of an extinct people. Yet it is one of my three names: as if a third of me was indecipherable.

The inscription on Bartlett Rees's gravestone is another mystery: 'I was dumb; I opened not my mouth because thou didst.' A reference to some kind of revelation, a religious conversion? Or was he incapable of speech? Deafness is a hereditary characteristic of our family. My father and my grandfather were almost stone deaf; my youngest brother – a professional musician – is going deaf. I, fortunately, have escaped the problem. Was Bartlett Rees dumb because he was deaf? Is this why he is commemorated in every generation since? The dead, like Ozymandias, pose as many unanswerable questions as the living. But at least one knows that they do not change, that they offer the same messages I read when I last visited Molleston churchyard fifteen years ago. There are innumerable relatives of mine here on this side of Narberth Mountain, a plethora of Reeses and Shanklins and the Welsh they married – Jones and Johns, Owen and Bowen, Watkins and Gwatkins, Eynon and Beynon. My great-grandparents, William and Esther Rees, are here in an unmarked grave: all I know about them is that he was a shepherd, that they, too, died in Narberth Workhouse, and that they were so tall no bed was big enough for them; for the thirty years of their marriage they put chairs at the end of their bed to accommodate their feet.

There are more of us in this graveyard than there were fifteen years ago. The two cousins I knew best, Arthur and Patty, are recent arrivals, Patty in 1979, Arthur in 1982. They were brother and sister and they lived in a cottage called Peter's Finger. Neither of them married.

Arthur, who was wounded in the Second World War, was a parish councillor, a deacon of the Baptist church, a rugby player, and he sang in the Whitland Male Voice Choir. 'Coy-er' he pronounced it. He was well known and much loved – a carpenter by trade, and general odd-job man to the whole district; he also farmed the three fields adjoining Peter's Finger. I remember leaning on a gate with him in a hot summer dusk, the air heavy with the scent of flowers and the drone of insects: we were sharing a companionable silence, chewing blades of grass and gazing at his cows. Eventually he scratched his bottom and said, 'Farming's very creative. But it's time to go to the pub.' More than any of the cousins he seemed to convey a sense of what our ancestors must have been like, to be a symbol of South Pembrokeshire man. His very existence spoke volumes to me. I loved and admired him – his slow, lazy grin; the Dylan Thomas blubber face and black, curly hair; his unhurried, unvarying geniality.

Why didn't they marry? Their sister Lily says Patty, when young, had several boyfriends, but she couldn't ultimately be bothered with them, and Arthur was always afraid he wouldn't find the perfect woman. 'I used to tell him she doesn't exist,' Lily declared. 'You only find out what she's like when you start to live with her.' Were they gay? I have no idea. But in this wealth of relatives I cannot be the only one who is. One in ten. If they were it was doubtless kept very hidden. They did not grow up in an age when such matters were discussed, let alone openly acknowledged; and in rural, conservative Little England Beyond Wales, where everyone knows everyone's business, it would still be impossible to be out. There is no gay pub or disco, no organization or switchboard, west of Swansea; Pembrokeshire and Carmarthenshire are gay deserts. I don't recall that Patty or Arthur had any special friends; perhaps if they were gay they didn't even admit it to themselves.

Patty Rees, one of the most intelligent people I've ever met, had a prodigious, jackdaw-like memory – she never forgot anything that was said to her. She had an insatiable curiosity about people's doings, occupations and preoccupations; she was enormously interested in the family, and knew the dates of birth of the most remote cousins she hadn't seen for decades and who lived in what were to her very distant parts of South Pembrokeshire – Marloes, Pembroke Dock, Angle. She much enjoyed a day out, and I would drive her to the beach, or Haverfordwest, Fishguard or Aberystwyth; for her these trips were a luxury, and she would always don her Sunday clothes, which included a hat some forty years old. Boredom, I guess, was her problem. She never had a job. Arthur earned the money, and she supervised Peter's Finger and him.

How many gay men and women are buried in this churchyard? Another secret the dead will not yield up. It is quiet here – beautiful and comforting. As churchyards often are. I like their certainties and their riddles. This is a family characteristic: my grandmother found them utterly fascinating, and would spend hours pouring over inscriptions, dates and rhymes. Years ago I took some roots from a clump of ox-eye daisies that were growing on Bartlett Rees's grave and planted them in my garden. They flourished, and when I moved house I dug them up and took them with me. They now bloom as happily in Stoke Newington as they did in Spreyton or Crockernwell, but the parent plant in Molleston is no longer here. Another secret – did it die, or did the sexton remove it? It is not important, but I'm sad that Bartlett's grave has no blossom now, even though I can read the inscription more easily.

Graves and their messages are important, despite Sir Thomas Browne's quoting many examples, ancient and modern, to prove that they are not. 'The iniquity of oblivion blindly scattereth her poppy,' he wrote in *Urn Burial*, 'and deals with the memory of men without distinction to merit of perpetuity. Who can but pity the founder of the Pyramids? Herostratus lives that burned the Temple of Diana, he is almost lost that built it; time hath spared the epitaph of Hadrian's horse, confounded that of himself.' Very true, and I love the rotund, sonorous seventeenth-century rhythms, but the dispassionate common sense of his reasoning leaves me cold. *Urn Burial* says nothing to me. Eliot in *Little Gidding* does –

We are born with the dead:
See, they return, and bring us with them.
… history is a pattern
Of timeless moments. So, while the light fails
On a winter's afternoon, in a secluded chapel
History is now and England.

Or Wales, where the light is failing too on this raw January afternoon and a thin, chill drizzle is beginning. We *are* born with the dead and they live on in us; they give us their faces, sometimes their voices, even their memories, so history is always now. That is the importance of tombs and epitaphs – and they also give dignity to the dead; their melancholy pleases; and their certainties and riddles enrich our lives. Our ancestors were, therefore I am.

I should like to be buried at Molleston, not too far from Bartlett Rees's grave: 'significant soil.'

I have tea with Cousin Lily. She is seventy; she has been widowed for thirty years; one of her sons died at the age of three, and the other edits a newspaper in Bath. She lives alone, but she cheerfully enjoys her life and her alone-ness. I have not warned her of my arrival: she recognizes me instantly; 'Oh, David! Come in!' as if we had last met yesterday, not fifteen years ago. The main topic of conversation is, of course, the family: who's died, who's been born, who's got married. We talk about Arthur, and the cancer that killed him at the age of sixty-seven. She says she can't imagine why her parents christened him with the middle name of Llewellyn – it's *Welsh*. 'It should have been James!' I mention his singing, and she says – which I didn't know – that she too used to sing, in the Templeton Ladies 'Coy-er.' 'But,' she goes on, 'I had to stop, see? Because of the pressure.' What pressure, I ask myself, thinking that perhaps the choirmistress didn't like her voice; she explains – 'high blood pressure.' Mrs Griffiths down the road had a similar problem, and it occurs to me that in any conversation I have with my Welsh relatives there is always a Mrs Griffiths lurking somewhere – a middle-aged woman one never meets who is overwhelmed by huge calamities: heart attacks or breasts lopped off, or she's been run over by a bus, dismissed from her job, or her daughter has disappeared with some wildly unsuitable philanderer. (We did have a relative who disappeared, Phyllis Howells, who ran off to join a circus and who got herself killed in an air-raid during the war.)

I make the usual promises to keep in touch – to write, to stay longer next time, to phone Ralph if I'm in Bath. I'm very glad to have seen Lily, for I have this strange feeling that the circumstances of life will prevent me from seeing her again. I recall Boswell's last meeting with Johnson; I 'sprung away with a kind of pathetic briskness.'

Little England Beyond Wales is not as cut off as it used to be – the man who owns the hotel where I stay overnight in Tenby is an Italian and the proprietor of the restaurant where I eat is a Scotsman. Next day I stroll round the town. It is so beautiful this windy January morning with not one tourist in sight, all the vulgar paraphernalia of modern seaside holidays packed up till June, an angry red sun beginning to peep through the clouds out to sea. I can just glimpse Lundy on the horizon. The whole sea's boiling: racing in over a vast stretch of sand that is completely empty except for two brave joggers in tee-shirts and shorts. Inside the ancient walls – pierced by five arches which, incredibly, wheeled traffic is still allowed to use – is the old town, picturesque as a postcard, magnificently preserved, gripping a windswept headland above a chocolate-box harbour full of boats and gulls. I would love to own one of these Georgian houses – in winter; in summer it would not be so pleasant. It is said that the Flemish colonists lived for the most part in Tenby and the surrounding area, that to this day Tenby people have a physical appearance distinctly different from the other inhabitants of South Pembrokeshire. I find myself looking at shoppers and shop-keepers to see if this is true, but I can't tell: what does a Fleming look like? Much like any other West European, I imagine.

The church is totally English. Only the names on the

plaques inside remind me that this is Wales. The stone commemorating Morgan Williams, the chairman of some business concern in Madras, informs us that he 'resigned the Presidency and his breath together.' Benjamin Rees, Bartlett's father, died here in 1805, but there is no memorial to him.

On my way home to London I stop at Laugharne, Llareggyb of *Under Milk Wood*, where 'time has ticked a heaven round the stars.' Its castle – the views from here of the enormous width of the Taf estuary are quite superb – marks the beginning of the Landsker, though Laugharne, strictly speaking, has nothing to do with Pembroke; it is just inside Carmarthenshire. There are Reeses in this grave-yard too, but I know nothing of them; and one's attention, naturally, is drawn to the most well-known incumbent – Dylan Thomas.

Laugharne on a grey wintry day is drab compared with Tenby; half-dead. I think of the people Thomas put into *Under Milk Wood*, and I hope that P.C. Rees, who in the middle of the night mistook his helmet for a chamber-pot, was not a relative. I don't care for *Under Milk Wood*, despite its intermittent flashes of genius – 'All my dead dears.' It's childish, its humour schoolboy lavatory humour.

As I reach Welsh Wales - Carmarthen and Pontarddulais - I ask myself why I have been to Molleston; why did I visit my relatives, the living and the dead? I really don't know. To find copy for my own version of *Urn Burial*, to see Lily Badham, to indulge in a bit of harmless ancestor reverence? To renew acquaintance with old haunts? All of the above perhaps, but there is something else too elusive to express. I can only come near to it by quoting again: Walter de la Mare's traveller –

> 'Tell them I came, and no one answered,
> That I kept my word,' he said.
> Never the least stir made the listeners.

I am also listener as well as traveller, hearing 'how the silence surged softly backward.'

Nobody in our family is famous. The nearest we come

101

to it is Jim Shanklin, who played rugby for Wales. There is one other published writer, Malcolm Bellamy. The Reeses on the whole followed the employment South Pembrokeshire had to offer, which was more varied than in other remote parts of the British Isles – farming, coal mining, the lime trade, ship building at Pembroke Dock. The shipyards (once the most modern in the world) and the collieries have closed long since, but oil refineries and the boats to Ireland have provided new employment. The Irish themselves came to Pembrokeshire in the last century to escape economic ruin. There was a distant ancestor called Caleb Murphy, carpenter, of East Williamston; and Florence Furlong's father, Thomas, was Irish, Catholic, and a well-known salt smuggler who 'worked' the Pembroke/Cork route. Some of his ancestors went to the United States to fight for the colonists in the War of Independence and settled there. Jim Bellamy, too, deserves to be spoken of; the only man I've known who fought in the Boer War. He was ninety-three when I last met him, physically frail, but as sharp in his wits as a youth. He described how in 1899 he cradled a dying friend who had been shot: 'I remember it as clearly as if it happened yesterday.' And a night ride of forty miles on horseback, carrying dispatches through enemy territory, 'expecting to be shot and killed every time I came near the Boers' camp fires.' He was blinded in both eyes by shrapnel, but recovered his sight in hospital at Dilfontein. He made it all live for me: his speech had a distinction of language that is rare now. Six months before he died his daughter, who never married and who looked after him for thirty years, went out to post a letter; she was found dead at the side of a road – a brain haemorrhage.

More employment opportunities though there were compared with Ireland, there was economic hardship in Pembrokeshire too; the deaths in the workhouse point to that. I don't know why my grandfather left Narberth Mountain for England at the age of sixteen, never to return, but I guess it was to find a job. His father died the same year – the breadwinner had gone. Also my cousins tell me he quarrelled with his mother. His brother Jack left with him and they found work in the stables of a colliery in Yorkshire. Jack Rees lived the rest of his life in the north of England, marrying Polly Tindall whose father was a painter of landscapes. She had been a maid in Queen Victoria's household. A 'good' marriage financially, I think. Grandpa did not stay long at the coal mine. He came south, to Norfolk, where he met his future wife, and then to London, where he worked as a tram driver. He died in 1948. He was born in the era of the horse and buggy and died in the era of jet aeroplanes; he could never, I'm sure, have imagined as he toiled in the stables that all his grandchildren would obtain university degrees. Or that one of them would write about him.

It's a kind of amends, this. My other grandparents have appeared in my books – Sarah Ann Rees in *Landslip*, my mother's parents in *Miss Duffy Is Still With Us* – but not James Rees. My mother, too, felt she'd neglected him. She told me once of a vivid dream she had had shortly after he died; he was frantically knocking on the window of our larder, and for some reason or other she couldn't or wouldn't let him in. She felt so guilty about this that she had a Mass said for him, which he would not have appreciated, being a Baptist.

Perhaps he is why I returned to Little England Beyond Wales; it was for him I quoted de la Mare: 'Tell them I came … that I kept my word.' And for him the silence surged softly backward.

LIFE IN VENICE

He had started to feel unwell before the plane left Heathrow, which was perhaps not surprising as take-off had been delayed for three hours: no explanation (as usual), no apology, no vouchers for meals or drinks. Airlines treated passengers like shit these days. All they were interested in was herding you into the departure lounge – so that they knew you were in a place you couldn't leave either to continue your journey or to return to wherever it was you were coming from – then abandoning you to tedium and starvation. (He didn't know it then, but the flight home would be worse – an unexplained *four*-hour delay in the departure lounge at Venice, which had no bar, no restaurant, no duty-free shops: nothing on sale, not even a newspaper; the only facility was a loo.)

The first sight of Venice cheered him a little. They strolled, the four of them, from the Piazzale Roma to the canal, and there it was - the city of our dreams and our imaginations; gondolas bobbing on sparkling water, the wash of boats breaking against the walls and stairs of palaces, the glitter of reflected light on stone. The activity of it all! The milling crowds of tourists, the noise of water traffic, the unceasing movement, the buildings assailing one's eyes like a thousand visual missiles, each clamouring for attention! And it was warm: a beautiful spring afternoon. They booked into their hotel, which was near the railway station, and gratefully abandoned their luggage; then boarded the number one vaporetto, which took them the entire length of the Grand Canal to St. Mark's. He began to feel queasy again before they reached the Rialto: a sliding in the stomach, headache, and a peculiar tightness in the lungs which made breathing difficult. He felt as if he was gasping for air.

The visual missiles became too much to withstand. There were so many of them; they hurt the eyes. It was like attending a banquet of sticky, over-rich cakes and being forced to eat every one. The sweet icing, the sugar-coating, was as rotten and stale as Miss Havisham's wedding breakfast; walls were cracked as if an earthquake had struck; stone stairs – built to receive gorgeously dressed noblemen, bankers and shipping merchants arriving in their gondolas – were no longer reminiscent of Canaletto or Guardi, but were disused, crumbling, slippery with green weed; damp dripped from dilapidated brick; towers, awaiting collapse, leaned at grotesque angles; the bottoms of doors, swollen and eaten by lagoon water, would never open again. Ground floors, even first floors, all seemed forlorn. He remembered *The Aspern Papers*, but the Venice of Henry James, where a perfectly delightful palace could be rented for a few shillings a year, had disappeared without trace.

Would James recognize it at all, he wondered as they stared at the colonnades in the Piazza San Marco – the stone that needed cleaning, the annoying flocks of pigeons, the barbarian hordes of tourists clicking cameras, the tatty, trashy, over-priced souvenirs on gaudy stalls that jostled for space by the cathedral's steps, that even obscured the walls of the Doge's Palace itself. La serenissima was now an utterly inappropriate name: there was nothing serene about this Venice of noise, bustle and bad taste. It was the cameras that irritated more than anything else. Every stone of the city, it seemed, was being photographed hundreds of times a second. These millions – zillions – of feet of Venice on celluloid in albums all over the world; what on earth was the point? The sterile passion to record; what did it give the takers of the photographs other than evidence to friends and family and neighbours that Peter Ivanovich Bobchinsky had been there? The camera always lies. It snaps the most fleeting of moments, presents it uninfluenced by what is before and after, extracts from the ever-rolling stream a single drop – and endows it with bogus significance because what is before and after, the stone or water or light beyond the edges of the photograph, does not touch it. It distorts what is really remembered. Has man no belief in memory, that diary, as Miss Prism said, we all carry about with us? Does he prefer the celluloid lie to the living truth?

Why am I so down, he asked himself. Venice was a challenge to gay men: the city of Symons and Corvo, Britten and Pears, Housman, above all of Tadzio and Aschenbach. It was, for gay men, a symbol of death. Was this why? He wanted to go to the Lido to see if it resembled Visconti's beautiful pictures of the dying Dirk Bogarde; but it would be as well to leave that journey to the last possible moment: one should not tempt fate. No, it wasn't why. The fact was he was ill, and his depression was the result of fear that illness would ruin a holiday he had been looking forward to for weeks.

The Byzantine gloom inside St. Mark's did not lift his spirits; the sombre gold and deep blue mosaics, though they were – it was obvious – superbly well done, reinforced dejection, oppressed with their unsmiling solemnity and commands to be discreet, virtuous and grave. The vistas between the columns were dark, and the dull red glow of sanctuary lamps did not illuminate; it added to the religious stuffiness, confirmed what this building said: not come unto me but, to all save the elect, keep out. He sat in a pew, again unable to breathe easily, while his friends wandered off, exclaiming at the delights unfolding in each new chapel, in each hitherto unnoticed mosaic. The voices of the crowds rose into the central dome and were dispersed, returning to his ears as a mumbled, disturbing jumble of meaningless whispers.

Outside, light stabbed; its intensity seemed to crack his skull. In the Doge's Palace he felt faint, had to sit again – in the Senate Hall – while the others explored the dungeons. The word stuffy came to his mind once more: and grandiose, grandiloquent, grande dame – it was a monument to too much spare cash and not enough artistic judgement. The paintings, which seemed to cover every ceiling and wall, filled every nook and cranny, were the products of the great and the good – Titian, Tintoretto, Tiepolo, Veronese, Bassano and so on – but all were second-best, left no clear impression, were a blur of hastily conceived gods and goddesses, staircases, pillars, robes, cloaks. For a thousand years the business of the Most Serene Republic had been enacted in this room: the downfall of Saracens plotted, sea battles planned, treaties, alliances and the annexation of territories argued, but mostly trade – what could be acquired cheap and sold dear – had governed all thought. The last doge, Ludovico Manin, on the twelfth of May 1797 had put his signature to Napoleon's ultimatum that dissolved the Republic and handed Venice to Austria as a sort of present. What was here now? Nothing. Nothing. Hic jacet pulvis, cinis, et nihil.

The cameras clicked and whirred.

They decided (or rather, the others decided and he went along with it) to round off the tourist day by going to Murano, a brief trip by vaporetto. He glanced, as they crossed the Bridge of Straw and followed the Riva degli Schiavoni, at the Bridge of Sighs, and deemed it inferior to its namesake in Cambridge, over which no prisoner had been dragged to inquisition or curtailment of freedom. And Venice was not a city for cripples, he thought as the steps up the bridge made him choke – his companions looked at him in surprise – and, struggling for air, he noticed that every bridge had steps. A man, transporting a cooker and two washing machines, had to bump them up on a cart, then, on the other side, bump them down. He felt a slight improvement when they were on the water; he could breathe more easily. The cut through the Arsenal showed pleasing depths of murky green canal, the sun shimmering on brick, trees and weeds flourishing in the derelict shipyards. But Murano turned out to be a very boring island. The others lingered over glass in the shops, watched glass being blown, bought glass; but he sat out of the heat on some dusty stairs where a building shaded him, and he said to himself, what is wrong with me? There were red-hot knives in both his lungs.

Back at the hotel he lay on his bed – his friends had gone out to eat, but the thought of food disgusted him

– and stared at a notice on the door: IT IS FORBIDDEN IN THE ROOMS TO WASH CLONES. He knew there was something incorrect with the English of that, but he couldn't decide what it was. The whole trip was a mistake: he hadn't much relished a holiday with these three particular companions, but they had put the idea to him and he had for years longed to see Venice. Norman, middle-aged, cardiganed and addicted to tea, was amusing and entertaining, but one could never believe a word he said, and he was a poor listener. Then there was Noel, much younger, Norman's friend (though they were sharing a room and had been going around together for a decade, they insisted, against all evidence, that they were not lovers); Noel was selfish and queeny, demanding his own way the whole time – though he had no money he spent a fortune on clothes, two thousand pounds last year it was said. He got by on plastic. Lyndon completed the group. Thinking about Lyn sharpened the knives in his lungs. They were room-mates, and they needed, really, to put distance between themselves, not exacerbate a tension-filled relationship by going on holiday together. The best thing that could happen to his immune system, he had often told himself, would be if he and Lyn parted for good. Lyn, though he was sympathetic and kind, was a bully, a teacher who couldn't stop teaching; he drank to get drunk, and was as irresponsible as Noel where money was concerned.

He was shivering now, and his shirt was soaked with sweat. He faced what he'd been trying to avoid: his temperature had soared and he'd have to send one of the others to look for a doctor. He loathed the idea of being a nuisance, but, he began to realise, the problem was more than a cold or a chill, maybe more than a bout of flu. They returned at last, noisy from a day well spent, from wine and a good dinner; his memory of things happening in sequence stopped at the point when he said to Norman, who was the first to come in and see how he was, that he felt awful, that perhaps they should fetch someone. After that there were only flashes, a few lucid moments – Lyn talking to him quietly and holding his hand (in the

108

hotel? Or elsewhere?); Noel staring at him, embarrassed and silent; Norman fussing (did this actually occur?) as he was carried downstairs and out into the night.

Then gaps. Many gaps. But most vividly: he was in a gondola being rowed through the dark between tall, gaunt buildings. People's washing hung above. He remembered the sound of wood, creak-creak, creak-creak, creak-creak. The gondola was narrow and sinister and black, and narrow and sinister and black was its steersman; was this the ferry for which the one coin was fee? Who pays the ferryman? What was he called? He couldn't think at first, but it eventually came to him: Charon. This was the ship of death. Someone had said, Lyn he thought, that a gondola would be fastest; the canal to the Ospedale Civile couldn't be negotiated by other methods. A gondola direttissima.

How long he was there he didn't know. Two or three days? A week? Two weeks? He was unconscious much of the time, tubes sticking out of him, an oxygen mask over his face; Norman, Noel and Lyn, singly or together sat beside his bed, their expressions anxious. But there were hours when nobody was in the room. One morning he seemed to wake, to be aware that events happened in sequence, that he had memory. He didn't want to get out of bed – he didn't want to move at all. It simply felt good to be lying between white sheets in a blank white room, staring at the oblong of window through which the sun streamed and out of which he could see only blue sky. He lay inert – for hours? Days? – and was glad.

Lyn said: 'His immune system has been in a poor state for some time. He was aware of that – *I* was aware of that – before we discussed a holiday in Venice. But he wasn't, at his last check-up, technically a P.W.A. His T-cell count was all right – though he's been P24 antigen positive for at least a year.'

They were sitting outside a restaurant that overlooked a canal, having dined on zuppa verdura, escallope milanese of the tenderest quality, and a very satisfactory bel paese cheese. They were sipping the last of their third bottle of red wine. A caravan of gondolas came into sight, their black shapes emerging – mysteriously, it seemed – from the dark: a party of Japanese tourists photographing relentlessly. One of the gondoliers was entertaining them with a performance of *O solo mio*. He had a good voice.

'This place is magical,' Norman said. 'It's an ill wind: if Martin hadn't gone down with P.C.P. we'd be back in England, grumbling about the rain and Maggie Thatcher. But here we are, against the odds, dining magnificently on a hot spring night in Venice.'

'It's a great nuisance,' Noel said. 'I can't afford to stay any longer – I *have* to go home tomorrow. If I don't, I'll lose my job. Besides ... to be honest, I can't cope.'

'With what, dear?'

'AIDS. Fucking AIDS! Pneumocystis carinii ... death.'

They looked at him for a while, not answering. 'I have to go too,' Lyn said. 'I've missed the first week of term ... Deputy heads are considered indispensible, even if we know they aren't.'

'I'll stay,' Norman said, 'at least till he's out of hospital. It's easier for me ... self-employed. As for death ... he isn't going to die! He's totally recovered – he'll be on his feet by Monday or Tuesday.'

'Till next time,' Noel answered. 'Well ... if you're staying on, I shan't feel so guilty about leaving.' He smiled. 'Maybe ... you'll find it's good copy for your next novel.'

'Really, Noel!' Norman was shocked. But after a moment or two he laughed.

'He couldn't have had more care and attention if he'd been in England,' Lyn said. 'They have all the right drugs ... and the doctors and nurses are so efficient!'

'Did you imagine they wouldn't be? Why should we think *our* hospitals give the best treatment? With the National Health Service as it is ... We're in Italy, not Ethiopia!'

'Sorry. It was a racist remark ... not intended to be.'

'It's a nuisance,' Noel said again. He helped himself to the wine.

From far off they could hear the gondolier's voice: *Santa Lucia*. Norman sang with it; then Noel and Lyn followed suit – three-part harmony. 'Saint Lucy,' Norman said.

'A virgin of Syracuse. Killed during the persecution of Diocletian. Her bones are said to be here in Venice, in the church of San Geremia.'

'Noel's right,' Lyn said, 'though I admit it grudgingly because it's a wicked thing to say. It *is* a nuisance. I remember telling Martin it would be, last New Year's Eve. I shouldn't have said so ...' He grinned. 'But I was drunk at the time. And I did add that we'd all rally round.'

'No one is sympathetic when you're ill,' Norman said. 'However ... it's enabled me to see a lot more of Venice than I would have done and ... I must say ... not one stone of it is a disappointment. Every square and church and street, every canal and bridge – some charming, unexpected view; and, away from the Grand Canal and St. Mark's, it's so peaceful! You don't realise, until you've been here for a while, the blessings to the spirit of somewhere that has no *cars*. The slower pace, the lack of noise, and I positively *bloom*, dear! Nothing's been torn down to make way for shopping malls and garages and what planners blithely think are "road improvements." I haven't seen a supermarket since I've been here. Wonderful! Little old shops just devoted to selling cheeses ... They give you a bit to taste before they cut your quarter kilo off some *huge* gorgonzola ...'

'I *adore* a big supermarket,' Noel said. 'I can't wait to get back to Sainsburys in the Holloway Road! A bit of hustle and bustle!'

'Philistine. You know, as well as the quiet, I love the *camp* in Venice. The Fenice is the only opera house in the world at which you arrive by gondola. Now ... you can't get more camp than that, can you?'

'Queen.'

'I'd like to live here. I think I probably will.'

Two young men and a woman walked by, their voices loud, accents jangling. 'You can always tell an American girl,' Noel said, 'by the braces on her teeth. Why do they go in for it? Nobody else does.'

'You can always tell an American man,' Norman said. 'Apart from the Israelis, they're the only nation that circumcise their cocks.'

111

They laughed. The wine was drunk; Lyn signalled for the bill. 'I feel bothered, going home without Martin,' he said. 'But ... what can I do? In some ways he has a very good immune system ... better than mine. I don't remember when he last had a cold, and he's never had flu in his life.'

'You're not to worry about a thing,' Norman said. 'I'll see he's O.K. I can manage.'

Yes, yes, yes, he assured Norman, he was all *right*; he was fit and well and didn't need mothering: Norman could fly back to England with a clean, clear conscience. He wanted to be alone for a while and in such beautiful April weather explore Venice – he hadn't so far had a chance to do this. When Norman stepped onto the airport bus in the Piazzale Roma, he felt an immense relief. Norman was kind and well-meaning, willing to give of himself in a way that Lyn found hard and Noel impossible, but he did *fidget*. And twitch. Like an old mother hen.

Happiness began at the moment when he waved good-bye, turned, and walked through the gardens to the Grand Canal. Sun and heat kissed his face. The canal, busy with gondolas, vaporetti, water taxis, barges loaded with goods, and shouts, curses, laughter, seemed a delight; how could he ever have thought it depressing, assaulting him with too many missiles? He leaned for half an hour on the parapet of a bridge, content to do nothing, just be. He was alive. He was in Venice. It was all that mattered. The relief. The *relief*! Alive! He would, he knew, become sick again — P.C.P. inevitably struck twice: then a third time, a fourth, until it killed you – but now at this moment, it was irrelevant. Just to exist was a sensation of pure joy!

He took the vaporetto to St. Mark's, then crossed to the lonely islet of San Giorgio Maggiore. The day's mist was not quite burned off; the effect on distant buildings was to render them insubstantial and dream-like, not as if they were dissolving: but forming, being made for the first time in their own Eden. The city was a symphony of water and stone, Turner's *Regulus* or *The Decline of Carthage*, Claude's *Seaport at Sunset*; light and in motion and thronged: steps, towers, spires, boats, quays, people, lapping waves, so essentially dependent one upon another it was almost impossible to tell where a particular shape finished and the next began. Was that a stairway rising out of the water or the water itself? The shifting, flickering patterns of light on the surface texture of stone and canal blurred distinction, fashioned their own illusions of turrets, cupolas, bridges, wharves: how the perspective changed as the boat swept into the open lagoon beyond the mole! In a matter of seconds campanile, Piazzetta, the pink icing of the Doge's Palace, even the clustered domes – a huddle of Bedouin tents – of St. Mark's were shrunk, were made to assume their rightful places as subservient to the power of water, and their rich colours dimmed in the olive green of the lagoon, which was thick like olive green paint, like olive green mud, flecked in the wash of a passing barge or gondola by the most subtle tinctures of grey or blue or white.

The sun blazed a dancing, dazzling gold path from the boat to Santa Maria della Salute; he stared into it until his eyes were sightless and this most Turner-ish, most Claude-like of basilicas was a one-dimensional black silhouette; the boat chuntered on and the Salute emerged from the blinding glare, solid now and grave, dimensions restored, domes moving into the places where quiet San Giorgio Maggiore would expect them to be. No one else got off the vaporetto: it was too early for tourists to venture this far. He looked at the stark, cream-coloured façade of the church, the ochre of the monastic buildings, and thought: I love this – its simple symmetry.

Inside was a delight too; Palladio's imposing intentions still clear and white and uncluttered, the only artefacts some of the finest canvases Tintoretto painted. The good taste in almost every Italian church! The sense of proportion, the absence of fuss and cheap tinsel, compared with Czechoslovakia, Austria, Portugal, Spain! No Baroque excess here; just classical line and curve, the correct width, the right height! He listened to the basilica's whispering silences and said: I'm alive.

113

Four days of pottering in narrow streets, nipping into churches, travelling by vaporetto, eating good dinners, drinking wine, and sleeping the clock round. The paintings: Bellini madonnas, Giorgione's strange, melancholic *Tempesta,* more swirling Tintorettos, Titian's moonlit *Pieta,* and, most striking of all, Veronese's *Last Supper,* which scandalised him it was so arrogant, then made him laugh with approval. Even the Piazza San Marco seemed less gaudy than on that first day when he was ill, and, though he felt he could never like it as he did the rest of the city, he found he was agreeing with the old cliché that it was a theatre, with the crowds in it acting the seven ages of man. He went into St. Mark's; it was Maundy Thursday, and Mass was in progress, so sightseeing was restricted: he sat at the foot of one of the pillars and gazed at the mosaics; uncompromising they still were, but his initial judgement that they were gloomy he decided was wrong – the gold glittered in the Easter sunlight, and the severity of form was softened by the radiance in the faces. The music accompanying Mass was annoying – an aimless plainchant improvised on the organ, a kind of Gregorian muzak – but there was a plethora of smells and bells, copes and mitres, Catholic camp: during the final cortèging around the nave he was somewhat embarrassed – and pleased – to be blessed by none other than the Cardinal Patriarch himself. A future pope? John the Twenty-third and John Paul the First, he reminded himself, had been Patriarchs of Venice.

On Easter Sunday he went by boat to the smaller islands in the lagoon. The weather, though still hot, was hazy, the sun only for brief moments penetrating the overcast. The water was no longer green; it was mud brown, the sludge colour of puddles, but its texture was still as thick as paint. Towards the horizon the brown gradually changed to grey, the grey of gulls and ships, then a lighter hue that was glassy, almost opaque, and in which the crooked wooden poles that marked the channels seemed like black Dracula stakes and, because of their reflections on the still, sombre glass, double the size they really were. The mysterious cemetery island and Murano, which looked no more alluring than it had done before, he decided to skip: Burano, its church tower leaning more spectacularly than Pisa's, and Torcello were his destinations.

Under the tower he said to himself: it will hurt no one when it falls – it will drop into the lagoon. Burano was pretty, like a miniature Venice; canals, coloured buildings, tourists, boats. The Venetians, he decided, must have *thought* water, unlike the rest of the human race who thought land, and in consequence built roads and vehicles with wheels: the Republic, concentrating on sea routes to Cyprus and the Eastern Empire, had turned its back on Italy for a millennium. What caused the long decline? Other modes of transport? The Turks? The collapse of Byzantium? A shift of power to Spain and England, trade with the Americas? Probably all of these things.

Torcello produced another surge of happiness. On this, the most remote island, there were very few houses, just green fields and silence. And an austere seventh-century church, silent too, with a Byzantine mosaic portraying *The Last Judgement*, in the centre of which was a beautiful resurrected Christ. When he came out the sun was shining. He lay on the grass and thought: this Easter I'm resurrected too. I'm well. I'm alive! But the following afternoon, his last before returning to England, he felt some trepidation – he took the vaporetto across to the Lido to keep his appointment with ... with what? The ghosts of Aschenbach and Tadzio? With death in Venice? Simply ... to keep his appointment.

It was a modern seaside resort, more attractive than some, with – he was surprised – roads and cars. The tide was out: the fringe of waves almost too weary to curl and break, and when it did its disintegration was a distant rustle. The beach was deserted. There were no bad feelings here. No Aschenbach in his deckchair, the henna running down his face; no Tadzio, angel of death, wading out to sea, beckoning. There was nothing here. Nothing.

He walked along the sand for half a mile to where there were people; he scooped a hole in a dune, stripped off to his knickers, and lay on his back to enjoy heat and sun.

After a few minutes he realised that every person on this part of the shore was male. He had stumbled, by chance, on the local cruising area. Yes ... the time-honoured rituals were the same as anywhere else; the parading up and down, the long looks, the pretence of absorption in a ship out at sea or some shells on the sand. He sat up and watched. Pretty boys, hairy macho men, queens. And a sprinkling of sexy, muscular, fit young men. One of the latter, wearing only brief swimming trunks, circled round him several times. Stopped at last and stared at him, then stared intently at his own toes. Stared at him again. Martin smiled, acknowledging. The youth, unexpectedly suntanned for this early in the year, came over and sat beside him. He was about seventeen; no older. Nothing was said, but fingers were soon stroking skin, and gentle kisses were exchanged; the last clothes were eased off. It was good to be nude in the open air, in the wind, to taste a sweet, salt body. With their hands they slowly brought each other to orgasm. And lay together for a while, just breathing.

On the plane, London-bound and exhausted (he'd overdone it), he said to himself, on the Lido I found a warm, living human, as warm and living as I am. I am. I *am*!

For a while.

SLEEP

What was Benjamin Britten's problem? None of the biographers, so far, has explained it: a relationship – apparently loving, caring and creatively fertile – with another man that lasted almost forty years; yet the heroes of the operas are emotionally tortured and crippled, and the music is essentially the product of a tragic vision of life. That is the music's appeal, of course; I have only to hear a dozen bars of *Peter Grimes* and I am looking for the Kleenex. Is it solely a question of musicology? What? The influence of Mahler? The latter, I think, is more than a musicological question, for the footprints of Mahler in Britten go beyond music. The *Storm* interlude of *Peter Grimes*, for instance, quotes from the first movement, the funeral march, of Mahler's fifth symphony – the 'Death in Venice' symphony – and Britten makes no attempt to disguise his borrowing; indeed he draws our full attention to it, loud and clear, thundering it fortissimo on the brass: parallels of private pain.

But Britten is not all tragedy; not all storm and stress. There are moments that are profoundly serene, which are, for the most part, connected with night, with sleep. Sleep in Britten's music is invoked as the most blessed of gifts, a state of being in which life and energy are renewed, when calm is restored and reconciliation begins. Moments of great beauty. There are nightmares, admittedly, that shiver the pattern; the *Dirge* in the *Serenade*, the Wordsworth setting in the *Nocturne*. Most nightmarish of all is a vision of total absence of sleep, the last lines of the Wordsworth, which Britten regards as the ultimate horror:

... I seemed to hear a voice that cried

To the whole City, 'Sleep no more.'
('Sleep no more' is an echo, presumably also deliberate, of *Macbeth* –

> Methought I heard a voice cry, 'Sleep no more!
> Macbeth doth murder sleep.'

Macbeth: that play, more than any other of Shakespeare's, which occurs at night, when the foulest deeds are committed under the cloak of darkness, and the punishment meted out to the perpetrators is an inability to sleep.)

In the *Nocturne*, the nightmare is expunged in the Shakespeare sonnet – darkness is paradoxically 'bright days when dreams do show thee me' – and in the rich, sonorous writing for strings, the optimistic D flat major chords; and the most emphatic part of the music stresses the words 'heavy sleep.' The same process is at work in the *Serenade*; the vision in the *Dirge* of purgatory 'fire and fleet and candle-light,' the fire that burns and the whins that prick 'to the bare bane,' is destroyed by sleep, Keats's 'soft enbalmer of the still midnight' that enshades us 'in forgetfulness divine.' Death's second self that seals up all in rest, Shakespeare said; it unknits the ravelled sleeve of care. It does. It does. Not to sleep is nightmare itself, or so I have found in the rare periods of my life when I have been incapable of sleep – the waking at two a.m., three a.m.: he is not here; and the hours, the black, bleak hours that followed when I, stunned by loss, numbed by hurt, have read till dawn or walked the streets till dawn, a dawn in which spectres and fears, the nightmare and her foal, did not drown in the golden deluge.

It is the most intimate, the most tender and the most trusting of all states of being: to surface in the middle of the night and to find him asleep in one's arms, just quietly breathing, is the greatest of joys. In the days, not so far off and long ago as they sometimes seem, when I had lovers, I would curl round him, wrap myself round him, I, the protector; one arm between his neck and the pillow, the other on his chest or his cock or holding his hand, one leg pressed gently between his legs – and drift with him into sleep, and wake not having shifted all night, or, if I did shift and wake, he was still there, trusting me, my arms, my skin, my breath. It was a kind of ecstasy: chief nourisher of life's feast. Now I am so used to sleeping alone that another man in my bed would be a nuisance, an unwelcome invasion of my private space, and I would, I think, sleep badly or not at all.

It is a pleasure to see people asleep: two men in bed, still, breathing, the sheet over them in folds, as if sculpted: Henry Moore's *Underground Sleepers*.

Nightmare, fortunately, does not visit me often, but when it does it invariably poses a repetition of the same theme: I am back in the years before I was an out gay man; I am married and my children are very young – we have just moved to a new house (which is sometimes in a place where we used to live, but we didn't know the house was there) or to a house we lived in once, but which now looks strangely different. There is something terribly wrong with all these houses and we have no knowledge of that until we move in – the roof leaks, or there are other people living there already, or the whole structure is on the point of collapse. I have lived in houses that needed major repairs, but I don't think these dreams have anything to do with real worries about real houses falling down. They derive from fears that the structures of my life may collapse, are echoes of its structures that have collapsed: my marriage, all my men. And maybe a more buried, less definable fear that *I* may collapse – the fear of loss of memory, of the disintegration of the personality. Of death.

These are times when sleep, for some usually inexplicable reason, has failed to be a restorer, a balm of hurt minds, when it has been unable to

> Turn the key deftly in the oiled wards,
> And seal the hushed casket of my soul.

Britten's music here seems to go beyond the longing for sleep that Keats's words express; the music does not ache – it is as if the composer is already experiencing the joys of sleep. Alone, or with someone else? It doesn't matter. In the *Nocturne* he is with someone else, though perhaps merely in thought – 'But when I sleep, in dreams they look on thee.' That has the promise, however, of the lover, if he is indeed not there, on another occasion being in the bed with him. This music, like sleep itself, is a salve; it cures: Britten, one feels, is renewed, capable now of beginning a fresh masterpiece, and we, the listeners, are also healed, given new energies, new beginnings. I, having slept well and dreamlessly, am writing this on a bright, spring morning; I am listening to the *Serenade* and waiting for the prospective purchaser of my house to come for a third time and decide that the bowed kitchen wall is of little significance, that structures will not collapse.

More of a nightmare than any bowed kitchen wall is recent information concerning the progress in my body of the HIV virus. I am now P24 HIV antigen positive, which means the virus, after years of dormancy, is on the attack. I've been told by the hospital that if I can't be returned to antigen negative status I shall become ill within eighteen months. I am to be a guinea-pig: injections of interferon three times a week may stop the rot. I don't relish the thought of injections, and interferon can have unpleasant side-effects, but I've told myself I have no choice. Which is interesting – to me, at any rate – because, running parallel to and contradicting the instinct we all have for self-preservation, the desire to live out the usual three score and ten, the fear of the manner of death, is an urge (faint, but nevertheless there) for self-destruction. The king in Eliot's *Journey of the Magi* said, 'I should be glad of another death.' Another sleep: death's euphemism, so often inscribed on gravestones; 'at rest,' 'fell asleep,' 'asleep in the Lord' –

> Ah, past the plunge of plummet,
> In seas I cannot sound,
> My heart and soul and senses,
> World without end, are drowned.

– where the ravelled sleeve of care will never disturb me again. Not that Housman, in the lines I've just quoted, is thinking of death. In the next verse he writes:

> His folly has not fellow
> Beneath the blue of day
> That gives to man or woman
> His heart and soul away.

Yes; that too is a kind of self-destruction, a death, a sleep that is no salve and does not restore. I, by opting for interferon, am opting for life. For the time being.

Though I occasionally say I should be glad of another death.

I imagine I will sleep tonight despite the virus and even if the would-be purchaser of my house jibs at the kitchen wall. I promise myself an unstressful afternoon – I am going to a poetry reading at which I will listen to a public rendering of a poem my friend David Harrison has written about me and my antibody status, in which he compares me to the fourth horseman of the Apocalypse. It's a good poem. I shall chat with friends after the reading, and drink some beer. Tonight, when I'm bored with the television, I'll listen again, I think, to the final songs in the *Nocturne* and the *Serenade*, and read in bed a few pages of Joyce's *Dubliners*. Then put out the light, arrange myself foetus-fashion, and relax. Drift towards sleep. Not Yeats's twenty centuries of stony sleep that were vexed to nightmare by a rocking cradle, but Keats's sleep that 'throws around my bed its lulling charities.'

Despite the swollen glands in my neck and my groin I'll wake tomorrow, refreshed, partially healed: another beginning. Though why am I writing this? A consolation, a pacifier, a dummy? Like the inscribers of gravestones, am I not using sleep as a metaphor for death? Britten, perhaps, did too. The most powerful song he wrote was the last in *Winter Words*; Hardy's

E'er nescience shall be reaffirmed

How long, how long?

I am sure that Housman's foolscap of eternal shade is for me eclipsing the golden deluge –

the subterranean dark

Has crossed the nadir, and begins to climb.

THE LITTLE OLD LADIES
OF SIDMOUTH

and Axmouth, Exmouth, Seaton, Budleigh Salterton and other resorts on Devon's costa geriatrica were in fact of various sizes, of middle age, and were – anatomically speaking – not ladies; but that is what they were called by the gay community of Exeter, which liked to consider itself more *au courant* than its rural brethren. In the opinion of Exeter's dashing young, life in Budleigh Salterton – or Seaton, Sidmouth, Axmouth and Exmouth – was the kiss of death, and indeed the average gay age along the costa, though perhaps some twenty years lower than that of its straight counterpart (retired right-wing couples: quondam military, business or civil service – walking-stick shops made handsome profits) was about forty-nine. Young gays, if there were any, fled as soon as they could to the metropolis of Exeter to sample the joys of its one gay pub and its weekly disco.

But pink life on the costa geriatrica wasn't a desert. The little old ladies were rich in pink pounds. The lack of any social focus such as a bar was more than compensated for by a rewarding pattern of friendships, the exchange of party and dinner party invitations, the stable relationships that had endured for many years. Literally and metaphorically people cultivated their gardens, though if the summer managed a few fair days they fluttered down to Budleigh beach, which for a long time now – through an unspoken agreement between its devotees, gay, straight, male, female – had tolerated nudity. The little old ladies sometimes talked of 'the gay end' of the beach as if it was the Dunas Maspalomas; but there was no wild sex in the sand, just half a dozen naked gay men chatting to each other about the assortment of bodies, desirable and undesirable, they had trudged past on their way across the stones, or who of their acquaintance was unexpectedly sleeping with whom, which they often appeared to know more about than the sleepers did themselves.

August the thirty-first was special in gay Sidmouth's calendar, for it was Jerry's birthday. Jerry, the most well-to-do of all the little old ladies, owned – with his lover, Guy – a handsome, Gothic-style, early nineteenth-century house on the cliffs just above the town; from its windows and the terraces of its well-kept, old-established garden there were stunning views of the sea. Guy always threw a party on Jerry's birthday, but this particular thirty-first of August was extra special, for Jerry was fifty, and they were also celebrating a quarter of a century of 'marriage': their silver wedding. A drinks party, Guy decided, was too ordinary for this occasion; instead he asked twenty people to dinner.

Gareth was surprised to be included. At forty, he imagined, he would be the youngest man there. He did not know his hosts or any of the guests at all well; he had only just arrived in the district – from Exeter: a curiously backward progress, his younger friends thought. The move was the result of a seven-year love-affair that had gone sadly wrong, had in fact, he now realised, been poisoned from the start. He sold his Exeter house to erase memories (though he still worked in the city, commuting each day) and bought a cottage in Sidmouth – it would soothe, he felt. It did. The unexciting tenor of this ageing and sequestered vale of life calmed him; and the almost total absence of any contemporary seaside development, the lack of gaudy, modern beach razzmatazz, boosted his recovery. Sidmouth was a genteel, Victorian watering-place, sheltered by dramatic, shattered cliffs the colour of apricot, happy – as he was – to pause. As he strolled up to Jerry's and Guy's he noted with pleasure the grey perms and grey clothes of real old ladies, the securities offered by announcements of flower-arranging classes and the Conservative Party's end-of-season fête, the bright floral displays in pots and tubs, the year's last visitors – swimmers and wind-surfers – enjoying the final moments of summer. Wood-pigeons cooed in the trees. Leaves, as yet, had only a hint of brown, of crinkling.

He had been asked because Guy thought he would 'fit in,' and out of kindness – Jerry and Guy were well aware of Gareth's recent history, though he himself had not told them anything of it; they wanted to suggest that the loss of a lover was a good time to make new friends. Gareth found that he did know some of the guests at least by sight – occasional forays, he supposed, they had made to one or other of Exeter's venues – and that in some instances he shared with them friends and acquaintances; and one man he knew by reputation. This was Roland, the only really outrageous queen who lived on the costa geriatrica – to survive in such an environment these middle-aged, comfortably-off men believed in 'discretion;' the retired colonels and wing commanders, it was thought, would react badly to anything being 'thrust down their throats.' Roland, however, didn't care a damn about the opinions of straights. One morning, swishing as usual up Sidmouth's High Street, he was noticed from the top of some scaffolding by a group of building workers; 'Are you a fairy?'one of them, muscled, tattooed and ultra butch, called out. 'Yes!' Roland replied; then flapping a wrist, shrieked, 'Vanish!' And minced off to an ear-piercing chorus of wolf whistles.

The food, everyone said, was excellent. The vichyssoise – green pea with lashings of mint – was much praised, but the cries of ecstasy were reserved for the roast lamb and roast potatoes, the courgettes, broccoli and runner beans, the vintage claret; 'How do you do it?' was asked several times. 'Roast lamb for *twenty*!'

'Oh … she's been slaving over a hot stove all week,' Jerry said.

'Language, Jerry,' Guy answered, his voice reminiscent of Margot Leadbetter's, and when Jerry looked puzzled said, '*Pronouns!*'

'Talking of that,' said Mark, who was not strictly

speaking one of the old ladies – he worked in Sidmouth but lived in Exeter; he and Gareth tooted their car horns at one another, often twice daily, as they passed on the road – 'Nic told me he had an amusing time at his doctor's. He doesn't know if the quack's aware he's gay, so when he mentioned his lover in the surgery last week, he was very careful with his pronouns. One does, one doesn't ... like Princess Anne. At the end of the recital, the quack said, "Tell Carl to drop in and see me." Superb runner beans, Guy. Where did you get them from?'

'The garden,' Guy answered. 'Why was Nic at the doctor's?'

'Nothing to do with him and Carl being HIV positive.' There was an embarrassed silence: some of the guests considered it out of order to mention a man's antibody status at dinner; others thought it a breach of confidentiality, or they said to themselves, what can you expect from Mark? He's so indiscreet after a finger or two of wine, and he's an estate agent: not quite one of us. But they also knew he was a genius at his work, that he'd found terrific bargains for nearly everyone who was seated at the dinner table, including both Jerry's and Guy's de luxe mansion and Gareth's bijouette cottage. 'Nic and Carl are quite open about having the virus,' Mark went on, not so insensitive to the reactions he had stirred. 'They say the secrecy we all surround ourselves with when it comes to AIDS is wrong. The lying and cheating most of us go in for produce distress, pain and isolation. They say we'll only conquer the disease when we come to look at it as we do cancer or heart attacks. I think they're absolutely right. Where are they? I thought they'd be here.'

'On holiday,' Jerry said. 'Gallivanting in Bled and Split.'

'From what *I've* heard, dear,' said Roland, 'I'm amazed young Carl hasn't bled or split. Lucky young Carl.' This caused a great deal of amusement; cock size was always a more acceptable subject for conversation than HIV status. 'But why,' Roland went on, 'if they're so frank about antibodies, doesn't their doctor know they're gay?'

'New doctor,' Mark said. 'Newish.'

'Oh. Well ... the other day I heard a particularly horrible

example of keeping quiet about AIDS. Two mutual friends of ours – '

'No names,' Guy pleaded. 'No names! It's not fair on them.'

'In that case, dear, I shall call them Mr A' – Roland flicked one wrist, then the other – 'and Mr B. *So* ... Mr A, knowing he was HIV positive, met Mr B and screwed him *rigid* ... some four years back. They've been lovers ever since, and Mr A has not revealed to Mr B that he has the virus.'

There were cries of protest from several people: such behaviour was a disgrace, inhuman, beyond all comprehension. 'You can't call them lovers,' said Patrick, who had a mouthful of Esther Rantzen teeth and was Jerry's and Guy's nearest gay neighbour. 'You don't love someone if you do that to him!'

'True, dear,' said Roland, pleased to have made such an impact and caught everyone's attention, but his triumph was spoiled by Gareth who suddenly spluttered on a forkful of broccoli, then pushed back his chair and ran into the kitchen for a glass of water.

'He's not one of them, is he?' Mark asked.

'Certainly not! Definitely not! That was just a coincidence.' He waited for Gareth to return, then said, 'The question is ... what does one do about it? If anything.'

'Do?' Richard, the oldest man present, a retired bank manager, echoed in mild astonishment. 'One does nothing. It is not one's business.'

'Hmmm,' Roland said. 'Though I guess I shall do nothing. Despite thinking Mr B ought to know. I feel by staying silent I'm ... I'm almost part of a conspiracy to murder.'

'Conspiracy to murder!' Jerry exclaimed. 'That's rot! Absolute tommy rot! When did you say they first plunged into the sack? Four years ago?'

'May 1985.'

'By then we all knew quite a bit about AIDS. That it was a virus; how it was transmitted; how to protect oneself. If Mr B let Mr A do the fucking minus a condom, and subsequently found he's HIV positive too – all I can say is it's his own fault. *He* has to bear at least some of the responsibility.'

There were general murmurs of agreement with this view of the matter. Guy signalled that the discussion was at an end by loudly asking if people wanted more wine and saying, 'Open another couple of bottles, Jerry.'

But, his glass refilled, Mark wouldn't leave it alone. 'Most venereologists employ a claptrapper,' he said. 'Why don't – '

'A claptrapper!' said Richard, who had not once in his sixty-five years needed to explore the inside of a special clinic. 'What on earth is that?'

'If you have the pox the quack will inquire about your most recent sexual partners, and, if you feel that it would cause horrendous difficulties to inform them, he sends someone round – the claptrapper in common parlance – to tell them they may be infected and should therefore have a check-up. But it's *not* done with HIV. I think it should. Oh, I can understand why not … if people didn't think their doctors kept HIV status as secret as a Roman Catholic priest keeps his parishioners' sins, then they just wouldn't come forward to be tested, and … also … no doctor relishes the idea of telling a patient he has some life-threatening virus that is, so far, incurable.' He drained his glass, and Guy, thinking the best way to shut him up would be to make him drunk or at least incoherent, quickly filled it again. 'There *are* promiscuous men who take no precautions,' Mark went on. 'Not gays so much now as bisexuals who know they have the virus and haven't told their girlfriends. And the clinics can do nothing about it! I heard of one instance; an HIV positive bisexual whose wife doesn't know and she's seven months pregnant. But their *doctor* knows.'

'Real estate, dear,' Roland said, '*does* have its exciting side!'

Everyone laughed, and Guy took the opportunity to remove the dirty plates and announce the sweet. 'Chocolate mousse with chestnuts and raspberries!' This had the desired result; the subject changed – everyone spoke appreciatively in anticipation of such divine decadence, and, in reply to the question of where he had found raspberries on the last day of August, Guy, who had hoped he wouldn't be asked that, admitted they came from the freezer.

But Roland fanned a guttering flame; he couldn't bear that Mark should have the final word. 'I know an example,' he said, 'that is just as bad.'

'Roland, do we have to?' Jerry asked.

'After this I'll shut up. Let's call the person Miss Z ... she isn't really a miss; a he, but a she in practice – well, you all know what I mean. And let's say it took place in Sunderland or Middlesbrough; is that far enough off?'

'I was born in Middlesbrough,' Gareth said.

Roland groaned. 'All right then, *Hull*. Anyone born in Hull? No? *Good*. I hadn't seen Miss Z for years, but six months ago his lover rang to say he'd died of cancer, long illness bravely contended, that kind of thing. I was shocked ... he was only fifty-three. And a very nice man. *Anyway* ... it turns out it wasn't ordinary cancer; it was Kaposi's. But the *hospital*, yes, the *hospital* insisted no one should know it was AIDS-related because Miss Z was a teacher, and they were *terrified* of being mobbed by the Sun-type press looking for juicy stories and ignorant parents thinking you can catch it from lavatory seats. They should have told the *truth*! What about sexual partners Miss Z may have had on the side? Former lovers? Shouldn't *they* have known it was AIDS, so they could do something about themselves if they wanted to? We aren't even permitted, it seems, to die honestly!'

'I'd prefer not to be told,' Patrick said.

'Dizzy queen! That's head in the sand.'

'So what is one to do?' Mark asked. 'What are doctors to do, VD clinics, AIDS lines? Break confidentiality?'

'I really don't know, dear,' Roland said. 'But one thing I'm sure of is that the present system is not in a satisfactory state.'

But at least one satisfactory state for Roland was that he'd had the final word. Mark offered nothing new, and the conversation went on to the excellence of Guy's chocolate mousse, the evils of tabloid journalism – 'I haven't bought a paper since I retired from the bank,' Richard said; 'They never tell the truth: lies, lies, lies and damned lies' – and Sidmouth's biggest yearly event, the folk music festival, which attracted to the town, several people said, too many undesirable, drugged-to-the-eyeball hippies.

Coffee and liqueurs were not served at the table: the party broke up into small groups and drifted into the lounge, or onto the terrace to enjoy the night scents of the last summer flowers: late blooms of stock, nicotiana, sweet William. Gareth made a point of seeking out Roland when – for once – the latter was not holding court; 'I'm interested in your Messrs A and B,' he said.

'Oh?' Roland made the word sound as if it had four syllables.

'I have to ... mmm ... find out who they are.' Gareth was aware this could suggest something about himself that he'd prefer to conceal; was Roland to be trusted? He didn't know the man.

Roland was quick and intelligent. 'It probably doesn't look it,' he said, 'but I *can* be utterly discreet. People tell you things, saying don't breathe a word to a *soul*. But the things fall into two categories ... sometimes your friend really means it's confidential, but it may in fact be *do* tell everybody in town! This was confidential. If you're in trouble ... Mother Roland has a broad shoulder to cry on. Vodka and sympathy.'

Roland indeed literally did have broad shoulders, Gareth noticed. Was a big man, and, despite being blond, was incredibly hairy. When young he must have seemed – at first sight – most desirable in a butch sort of way. Perhaps that was his tragedy. 'Thank you,' Gareth said. 'I'll remember that. But ... I must know the names.'

Roland sighed. And told him.

'As I feared.'

Soon afterwards Gareth said goodnight to Jerry and Guy, and left. It was still early; he was the first to go.

'He didn't stay long,' Jerry said. 'Do you think he wasn't enjoying himself?'

'Odd,' Guy agreed. 'And that spluttering on his food when Roland was in mid-flight ... Was that significant?'

'No,' Roland said. 'He told me just now he has to be in his office at eight o'clock tomorrow morning. Work piling up ... and don't forget he hasn't recovered from his affair with that queen of a toy-boy, Hugh. What was his nickname? Daisy? Daphne?'

'Dora,' Jerry said. 'Yes ... you're probably right.'

'In that case,' Guy said, 'let's have some more cointreau.'

Gareth walked down into town and home, deeply disturbed. Life with Hugh had been very difficult. It seemed, looking back on their seven years together, that they had spent most of the time looking for viable alternatives to each other, but neither of them had been able to make a clean break: this had led to flings with various men. One fling, for Gareth, was with Roland's Mr A – in March and April, 1985; it had ended when Mr A met Mr B. The screwing had been superb: just thinking about it now produced a sharp pang of desire in his cock. Mr A's body was marvellous – at the time Gareth couldn't get enough of it. A great deal of sperm during those two months had slipped into all the usual orifices, both his and Mr A's, and with it perhaps – probably? Certainly? – a great deal of AIDS virus, for they had not once used a condom. He recalled Jerry's words at dinner, 'By that time we knew a lot about AIDS ... If he's positive it's his own fault ... *He* has to bear at least some of the responsibility.' It's *my* fault then, Gareth said to himself; I should have insisted on precautions. But he didn't, he reminded himself, know much about AIDS in 1985. The use of condoms wasn't, then, general practice in provincial, if-we-don't-look-it-may-disappear Exeter; AIDS affected other people in other cities, indeed other countries.

He was suddenly hit by a thought so nasty that he stopped in his tracks. Mr A, Roland had said, knew he was HIV positive when he met Mr B. *When* did he find that out? Did he know before he and Gareth had started screwing? In all those lovely, marathon struggles between the sheets he knew that ecstasy was an agent of death? The idea made Gareth feel so angry he felt he was quite capable of committing a murder.

He gazed out to sea and said to himself, I will have to have an AIDS test. He had no choice. His world, it seemed, was collapsing around him.

With such knowledge, how in the future could he act? Eddie: a glimpse in the pub of this youthful, slim man filled Gareth with lust, the urge to rip off clothes on the spot. He hadn't made his interest at all obvious; Eddie was involved with somebody else. But that was coming to an end, and the last time they'd spoken Eddie was more aware of him – 'I'm glad you've grown a moustache,' he said. 'It really suits you.' He'd planned, on the next occasion, to suggest driving back to Sidmouth for coffee. But if he had the virus? It would probably ruin his ability to operate at all as a sexual being. It might only work with others in the same situation, but how to find them? Roland and Mark had stated the truth: unnecessary bloody secrecy.

The nights were chillier now: summer's end. The weather forecast was rain and high winds, and the sea was more restless than earlier that evening. A light out near Teignmouth gleamed an instant and was gone; another at sea, a ship, flared briefly, then it too vanished. He walked for a while on the shingle, but the sound of stones sucked by the surf did not soothe, produced no answers. It never did.

He said aloud: 'The days are drawing in.'

BYZANTINE – ONE

It was to become known as the funeral oration of the Roman Empire, Constantine the Eleventh's speech on the evening of the twenty-eighth of May, 1453. For almost two months Turkish artillery had pounded the walls and weakened them fatally. Those walls had lasted a thousand years; no one in recorded history had breached them, not even in 1204 when the Crusaders had sacked the Queen of Cities. The Emperor spoke bluntly. There would be no surrender. Fight to the death. Be steadfast in the hour of trial. God was on their side; He would never allow the infidel to capture the sacred places. While the solemn and Orthodox rites were still celebrated in the cathedral of the Holy Wisdom the capital of the Empire was protected by God and His Holy Mother.

The more worldly in the crowd regarded this as non-sense. It had been foolish of Constantine not to accept the terms of surrender offered by the Sultan weeks ago. They were the usual terms: if the gates were opened and the Byzantines laid down their weapons, no harm would come to anybody. Rights of property would be respected, freedom of religious worship be allowed to all. The Emperor would be a Turkish vassal of course, and tribute would have to be paid. But if the gates were not opened, the city would be sacked; three days of plunder, rape and destruction – it was the law of Islam – would follow. The Turks honoured agreements. Many cities in the Empire had surrendered quietly and their inhabitants continued to live in much the same way as they had always done: taxes were taxes – paying them to a Turk was no greater hardship than paying them to a Greek.

Constantinople was different, however. If it surrendered, it would be the end of the known world. A thousand years of history would have been endured in vain. The more superstitious believed it could not fall; the ancients had prophesied that it would last beyond the end of the second millenium since the creation of the universe, the year 1492.

When the Emperor had finished speaking, the crowd made its way, as if by instinct, to Santa Sophia. Constantine also went, to pray and to hear for a while the chanting of the monks, to sniff the incense, to look at ikons that had shielded the city in previous calamities. He begged forgiveness for his sins; he received Holy Communion. These were the last rites of the Empire, though he did not know that.

He returned to his palace at Blachernae to say farewell to his household. It was a hot, still night, humid and silent. No sound came from the Turkish army camped outside the walls.

Andrew Chionides at eighteen was one of the Emperor's most faithful servants, fanatical in his devotion, his hero worship. Constantine was handsome and popular, the embodiment of the old ideal of the warrior king, brave, modest, decisive; indeed if somebody less charismatic had occupied the throne, there would have been a revolt when Mehmet delivered his ultimatum and the city would have surrendered. Constantine was in spirit a Caesar Augustus, a Justinian, a Basil the Second. But in fact he was the toy emperor of a toy empire which was bankrupt, exhausted, and squeezed into no more space than a half-ruined city protected by stout walls. Emperor might be his title; heir he might be to ten centuries of splendour, but he was no more than the mayor of a decayed market town that had long since lost any useful existence.

Andrew Chionides saw none of the realities of the situation; he was aware only of Constantine the man and the traditions he had inherited. Andrew's intelligence had led to scholastic achievement, not political awareness. He was devout, pure, and Orthodox; he hadn't yet decided,

133

but he hoped he would one day become a priest. The Emperor did not say so, but Andrew, he thought, had the mind of a future Patriarch. Physically he was a tough, well-developed youth, and so strikingly handsome that he inspired lust in many people of both sexes. He dismissed overtures from girls with polite words, from boys with laughter. At fourteen he had been much given to masturbation, but he had freed himself from what he knew was a sin: his body, as well as his soul, was dedicated to God. Some regarded him therefore as snobbish and aloof, a pious do-gooder who sucked up to Constantine; pride, they said, would have a fall. This, perhaps, was a misreading – Andrew was sweet-natured and generous. But he set too much store by behaving to the strict letter of the rules, and he was naive: he had no idea that his good looks and the Emperor's praise caused other servants in the Imperial Household to dislike him.

John Angelos in particular. When they were both sixteen, Andrew, one afternoon when he had no duties to perform, had been exploring some outbuildings of the palace, stables that had lapsed into ruin in the last century – no one had had the money or the desire to repair them. Much of the palace was in a similar state; long before the Turks began their siege a foreign observer reported that it was 'a blackened shell.' His curiosity aroused by strange noises, Andrew peered into a small, dark room. What he saw in there shocked him: six of the servant lads, including John Angelos, were indulging in a sex orgy. He fled, thinking he had not been noticed. But John had seen him. Andrew kept the information to himself for a while, but to be silent troubled him – a week later he told the Emperor.

Constantine, too, was shocked. And angry. The punishment for unnatural vice was death, but for hundreds of years no one had been sentenced to death for anything, let alone buggery. His aides advised castration, which had been, until relatively recent times, a common practice: though not as punishment; a liberal supply of eunuchs was considered beneficial to the workings of empire – it lessened sexual intrigue in the palace and helped to concentrate men's minds on more useful business, like running the government or how to repel marauding Bulgars, Serbs and Turks. It was a way of getting on. But Constantine employed few eunuchs; removing a man's genitals was in his opinion barbaric. So he decided that the culprits, because they had a taste for each other's organs of excrement, should be utilised as shovellers of shit: they were condemned to work in perpetuity in the imperial latrines.

They thought of nothing but revenge. John Angelos counselled them to exercise the age-old Byzantine virtues of patience, diplomacy and cunning. He had a plan: a machine to build, which though it required few materials (four blocks of wood and some metal bars) would take a long time to assemble, to test, to perfect. And even when it was finished they would have to choose their moment for its employment with the utmost care.

Constantine expected the Turkish attack to begin at sunrise, so his farewell to his staff was short; they should go to bed early, he told them – tomorrow they needed to be more wide awake than they had ever been. He was clutching the bag of dust Emperors always carried. It was to remind him that man was created from dust, and to dust he will return. To Andrew he said that if the victory was theirs, if the enemy was repulsed, a glorious future lay ahead: in the Empire's recovery Andrew would have a part, a great office of Church or State could eventually be his. What he had to do tomorrow was to fight well, be a true soldier. Andrew promised he would, and said that if he died he hoped he would die as a martyr to God. Constantine frowned: he did not want to listen to talk of death or martyrdom. 'The Holy Virgin will protect you,' he said, and he put the bag of dust aside, leaving it on a chair.

Andrew, alone in his room, prayed for nearly an hour. When he slept, he slept dreamlessly.

Constantine's last act before going to bed was to speak for a few moments to the Stylite saint who had set up house on the top of a column in the square outside the palace. Stylites had been extinct for centuries, but with the fall of Constantinople, in the opinion of some holy men, now inevitable, a few hermits had taken up residence on the tops of pillars in various parts of the city. Whether they imagined this would somehow give them sanctuary from the Turks, nobody knew; maybe they thought that in the event of death they would in such places be nearer to Heaven. If the Turks should be defeated, Constantine said to the saint, he would have a roof built on the top of the column; it distressed him that in last week's foul weather the holy man had been buffeted by hailstones. 'The moon is eclipsed,' the saint replied. 'Have not the prophets warned us the city will be destroyed in the days when the moon is put out? The great gold cross on the dome of the Holy Wisdom was suffused at sunset with a weird, reddish light. With blood and flame!'

'The reflection of the Turks' camp fires.'

'Emperor! Look to your bag of dust! The world is but dust that trickles through your fingers! Man has been taught he is nothing, so night must shut on his knowledge! A moonlit dome disdains all that man is! Emperor! Look to your bag of dust!'

Constantine turned, and went back to his palace. All saints, he had decided long ago, were a bit deranged.

John Angelos worked on his invention in a remote part of the palace ruins; another dilapidated shed. He took few precautions to conceal what he was about, but it is not a surprise that nobody discovered him. The city's population at the time of the sack in 1204 had been a million; since then it had declined to less than a hundred thousand. Whole districts burned by the so-called Crusaders had not been rebuilt; cornfields, dairy farms now existed where palaces, houses, shops had stood. The windows of churches were left broken, the lead stripped from their roofs. The money to rebuild was lacking, and so was the desire. The Great Palace had been abandoned in 1204; most of it had been pulled down and its timbers used for fires to bake bread. The Emperors moved into the smaller palace of Blachernae, but they could not afford enough staff to occupy the whole of it. It was possible in any quarter of Constantinople to work quite openly, like John, on some secret project and remain undetected.

What is a surprise is that Constantinople had lasted so long. The bezant, once the standard monetary unit of all Europe, had been devalued so often and by so much that it was a worthless joke. This city, the crossroads of commerce, had centuries ago been by-passed; Venetian and Genoese ships had moved the world's trade elsewhere. Constantine's great-grandmother, the Empress Anna, had pawned the crown jewels and the imperial regalia to the Venetian doge – the scavenging shark of Europe – to raise money for futile, dynastic wars that crumbled the Empire within. No one since had had the cash to redeem them. Replicas had been made of glass, and were used at coronations and on occasions of state, but they looked to everyone who saw them what they actually were – cheap imitations. Palace guests did not now eat from gold dishes (they, too, had been pawned) but from pewter or gold-painted glass. Nothing was what it attempted to be: it was all tawdriness and tinsel, the crown and jewels and dinner service of a child's play-box.

Yet this had once been the greatest city the world was ever to see, the repository of more holy relics than had been found in Palestine, a fantastic amalgam of cathedrals, churches, castles and palaces, whose richness had astounded the Crusaders: such marbles, ivories, enamels, mosaics, brocades, bullion, jewellery, silk, were unknown in the West. The Crusaders destroyed or stole most of it. Priceless works of art, whole libraries were burned, the jewelled backs of books being ripped off beforehand; manuscripts, centuries old, were lost for ever. Plays of Aeschylus and Sophocles, discourses of Aristotle, never to be read by a Westerner, may have been consigned by the looting Crusaders to the flames. In the Great Palace the throne that could be lifted up to the ceiling at the touch of a button, the clockwork lions that roared, the golden bees that flew, the golden nightingales that sang to keep a drowsy Emperor awake (some said more beautifully than real nightingales), were smashed to bits. The sack of Constantinople was the worst of crimes, almost beyond compare. 'Of the treasure that was found in the palace I cannot speak,' one eye-witness said, 'for there was so much that it was without end or counting. Never, since the world was created, had so much in a city been plundered.'

John was a descendant of one of those smiths of genius who had made the golden lions that roared; invention was in his blood. His machine for the punishment of Andrew Chionides was a work of art, magnificent in its simplicity and its subtlety.

When Andrew was wakened he thought for a moment it was a summons to get dressed and go out to the walls, that the Turkish attack had started. He soon knew that this was not the case: a sword was being held at his throat. 'One word and you're no longer alive,' John Angelos said. There were six of them; the six he had reported to the Emperor. They stank of latrines. He was dragged out of bed; his hands were bound, and he was taken away, barefoot and in his nightshirt, through the deserted, darkened corridors of the palace, out into the open air, across quadrangle after quadrangle until they reached the room where two years ago he had seen the orgy. A torch was lit. In the middle of the room was a strange contraption of wood and metal; he had no idea what it could be, nor what it could be used for. His hands were unbound. One swift cut of the sword ripped his nightshirt from top to bottom; it fell from him and he was naked, surrounded by six villains whose grinning mouths seemed like the embodiment of pure evil.

He was pushed against the strange contraption. A metal bar, a small semi-circle cut out of its middle, was lowered until it was just above the base of his penis. Another was raised until it met the first. They were then clamped together: it was most ingenious; if he tried to pull himself out he would lose his balls. His arms were pinioned at the wrists by two pieces of wood, like medieval stocks, joined together by another metal bar. His feet were placed in a similar device. A handle was turned, and the upper part of his body was pulled down; he was positioned like a clock at ten to seven. The thugs did nothing for a moment; they were proudly surveying their achievement. They could now thrash his buttocks to pulp, Andrew said to himself; that was what they were going to do: savagely beat him. He began to pray silently to the Holy Virgin for strength and courage.

He was wrong in his guess.

When the truth dawned on him, he felt it would be worse than being beaten to within an inch of his life; the physical agony would be less perhaps, but he had dedicated his body to God: it was a temple. Now it would be defiled; the humiliation, the invasion of himself, the mental torture, the emotional scars would be beyond endurance. He tried to concentrate entirely on prayer, on shutting out the horrible thing that was going to be done to him. But he was astonished, terrified and disgusted that the penis being slowly inserted into him produced not only pain but sensations that caused him to shiver with pleasure. When his attackers observed that he was erect too, they laughed and cheered; a few twists of the handle and his body was almost upright – they could now deal with him at the front as well as the back.

He longed to die. It would be better to be killed by a Turk at the walls.

He was raped maybe as much as a dozen times; almost as many times was induced to orgasm himself. Nobody counted. It might have gone on longer if the Turks had not broken into the city, as Constantine had forecast, at sunrise. None of them to begin with came near the palace, and when they did so they were not particularly concerned with exploring the stables. But the noise of battle – drums, trumpets, shouts, screams, blood-curdling yells, the thunder of horses' hooves, the clash of swords, the explosions, buildings crashing to the ground, the walls of the city tumbling into the moat – caused the thugs to quicken their operation. Most frightening was the boom of the huge cannon built for Mehmet by the Hungarian engineer, Urban, who had once offered his services to the Empire. Constantine did not have enough money to buy the Hungarian's invention, but the Sultan did. What was planned for the Byzantines to use against the Turks was being employed against them.

When the fighting drew nearer, the rapists put on their clothes and hurried off, leaving Andrew still imprisoned. He was free now to scream and shout, but all he could manage was a gurgling choke like a death rattle. He had fainted more than once during his ordeal; tears streamed from his eyes; his wrists, ankles, and sphincter were raw and bloody. The pain was excruciating. Eventually he was found by a party of Turks. For a while they stared in wonder; then they played with the handles, experimented with the locking mechanism, and more by accident than design they freed him. He fell to the ground. They could have killed him then and there, but they did not; he was obviously harmless, and the machine was of more interest than a naked Greek. They wheeled it away: it was, they concluded, a useful instrument of both torture and pleasure; Mehmet would be delighted.

The looting and destruction lasted seventy-two hours: it was the law of Islam. Thousands were murdered, men, women and children; others were sold as slaves. Houses were broken into and ransacked, churches gutted and their treasures burned or stolen. Ikons, books, paintings were thrown into the fires. Blachernae was demolished. The doors of Santa Sophia were hewn down with axes, and the vast crowd of people inside was slaughtered or dragged off to captivity. Screams and tears echoed round the dome of the cathedral where moments before it had been filled with the singing of the morning liturgy and the sounds of prayer. The gold and silver ornaments were carried away, the crucifixes were shattered, the most sacred ikon of the Empire – the Hodegetria, the Mother of God, protectress of the city, painted, it was believed, by St. Luke – was smashed to bits. Then, tired of breaking things, the Turks began to rape the women and the adolescent boys. Nuns in particular were selected, and the high altar was used as a bed.

The victims thought God would intervene, but He did not. It was the Sultan who intervened. He arrived at Santa

Sophia on the third day and gave thanks to God for his success. He extended his mercy to all who were left alive. The great cathedral church was now to become a mosque: all remaining Christian signs and symbols were to be removed, and the dazzling mosaics whitewashed out.

Important government officials were executed, but some escaped to the Genoese and Venetian ships anchored in the Golden Horn, and with others, more ordinary citizens who were lucky enough to be taken on board, sailed off to exile in Italy. Constantine was not one of them. He could not be found, which annoyed Mehmet – who wanted either to view the corpse, or if he was taken alive, to cut off his head. He was last seen at the Gate of St. Romanos, fighting valiantly as a common soldier; he had thrown away his imitation jewels and his bag of dust. So he was presumed dead, though it is possible he avoided capture and somewhere lived out his life in total obscurity.

Andrew eventually found enough strength to crawl out of the stables. His nakedness excited attention, but he was unaware of that: his mind had gone. He lived for a week on scraps of food he found in the gutters or in deserted houses, and he set up home on the pillar outside the ruins of Blachernae. The saint who had told Constantine to look to his bag of dust had disappeared. Andrew would stand on the pillar for hours and rave at the top of his voice, incomprehensible diatribes against God, the Emperor, the Sultan. He was quite a tourist attraction for the Turkish soldiers, but after a while they forced him to come down; nudity offended Allah. A loincloth wrapped round him, he lay on the steps of Santa Sophia, and begged, so dirty and matted he was almost beyond recognition. The Turkish authorities took him into custody at last: he had become a nuisance; there were complaints that he interfered with teenage boys. There was one obvious cure for that – they cut off his balls.

Some months later he returned to the cathedral steps, and lived there for years, begging for coins or food.

Of the six rapists, three were killed during the hours of

destruction and plunder, and two escaped on a Genoese ship. But John Angelos stayed and survived, indeed prospered. The Sultan was enchanted with the pleasure/torture machine and used it himself; Byzantine adolescent boys suffered in it for his enjoyment. If they resisted too strongly he sometimes, when he had finished with them, cut their heads off. He demanded that its inventor be found and brought to him. So John Angelos was given money and granted privileges; he became a convert to Islam and built a number of war machines that helped the Turkish army to conquer Serbia, Bulgaria, Wallachia, and the Empire of Trebizond. He grew rich.

He paused one morning outside Santa Sophia and tossed some coins to the beggar, the once handsome youth who would have become, had circumstances been otherwise, the Patriarch of Constantinople. John knew who the beggar was, though nobody else did, but the beggar was too insane to recognize him. John stared intently at Andrew for a moment, then shrugged his shoulders, and went on his way.

BYZANTINE – TWO

'Gay fiction and its current crisis' was the billing for BBC 2's *Late Show* on May 24th, 1989; 'a discussion with Edmund White and others.' The crisis turned out to be how we deal in our novels with AIDS, but if anyone was hoping for serious analysis of this subject – or indeed anything about gay fiction in Britain – they were disappointed. A filmed monologue by Edmund White on the history of gay fiction opened the proceedings; this was followed by a studio discussion with the same author, and David Leavitt and Tom Wakefield. During the monologue Edmund White read extracts from Christopher Isherwood's *A Single Man*, Alan Hollinghurst's *The Swimming-Pool Library*, and his own *The Beautiful Room Is Empty*; afterwards, he and David Leavitt so entirely dominated the discussion that Tom Wakefield had only one opportunity to say anything. So it wasn't gay fiction and its current crisis, at least as far as British authors were concerned; it was as if none of us existed, as if virtually no gay fiction is produced in this country, as if gay writing was an almost exclusively American affair. David Leavitt talked about his new novel, which is not on the subject of AIDS, and Edmund White said – amongst a lot of other things – that he and Adam Mars-Jones had written *The Darker Proof*. The Hollinghurst extract, the reference to Adam Mars-Jones, and the chairperson – Sarah Dunant – telling us that Tom Wakefield's most recent gay novel was *The Variety Artistes* (in fact the most un-gay novel that Tom has written) were the only moments when modern British gay authors were mentioned. It wasn't a serious consideration of gay fiction and AIDS, but a self-advertisement show by White and

143

Leavitt, two American authors who are both sufficiently hyped to need no puff from the BBC.

Francis King, Colin Spencer, Patrick Gale, Michael Carson, Peter Robins – to name just the first few British writers that come into my head – were not mentioned at all, nor were any of our publishers. Were these writers, and representatives from Gay Men's Press, Brilliance Books and Third House all unable to appear on the programme? I doubt it. The omissions, I would hazard a guess, were promulgated by a straight establishment not caring and not daring to acknowledge that we write books too. Gay novels can be discussed, they seem to think, if the authors are *American*: the exotic, the bizarre, and the unmentionable are O.K. if they're foreign; the products of a far-away culture unlike the home life of our own dear queens. Once again the impression is reinforced that being British and gay is only tolerable if it is kept out of sight. This is a deadlier weapon than overt persecution: the quickest way to kill anything – and that includes books and their authors – is to pretend that it isn't there.

When was a novel from Gay Men's Press, Brilliance Books, or Third House last reviewed in *The Observer* or *The Sunday Times*, indeed in any mass circulation newspaper? Has *any* novel from these publishing houses *ever* been reviewed in a mass circulation newspaper? We are seen as a minority interest, fit only for the ghetto, in fact more of a minority interest than almost any other: black writers and women get more coverage than we do. What, therefore, is so specialised about us? Nothing. We write, like any other novelists, about themes that are common to *all* fiction – relationships, love, death, sex, friendship, growing up, growing old, and so on – but because our characters are homosexual the straight world thinks us unworthy of consideration. As if we weren't quite human.

I don't particularly want to knock Edmund White, who is a pleasant and decent man, but I have to say that I don't much care for his books. All too often he disappears up the purple interiors of his metaphors; am I the sole reader of *A Boy's Own Story* who abandoned it after the first hundred pages, bored and deciding that life was too brief for this sort of thing? As for David Leavitt, he is very young and is as yet no more than 'promising,' having given us so far two novels and a book of short stories. Not, therefore, an expert. Tom Wakefield, on the other hand, is worth ten times as much as either of the Americans in experience and achievement, but instead of commenting on *Mates*, *Drifters* and *The Discus Throwers*, he was allowed only a word in edgeways. Now a discussion between him, Francis King and Colin Spencer *would* have been worthwhile. We might have learned, from a trio of writers who have produced a substantial body of work, something about gay fiction.

Almost nobody has yet written on the subject of AIDS, said Sarah Dunant; why not? Edmund White said the problem was you had to have a major character who has AIDS, and you therefore had to have a death; this could become monotonous and repetitive. Not so, of course. You can write about the social and emotional consequences of HIV infection, as I did in *The Wrong Apple*, without having a death; you can write about bereavement, you can write in all sorts of ways about the effects, both good and bad, that AIDS may have on the lives of people who do not have the disease. There probably won't be a vast corpus, in time to come, of AIDS literature as such – there are only two important novels, for instance, inspired by bubonic plague – but it is a subject for fiction like any other, a tool of the trade so to speak. But will it get published? One straight publisher said to me revealingly – and ominously – that no one outside the gay world was the slightest bit interested in AIDS or HIV, that it was impossible to market as a theme.

I don't think I'm unduly chauvinistic in objecting to Edmund White, an American, being hauled in as the guru when the BBC decides to give gay fiction an airing, nor an ageist in reverse when I question whether someone as youthful as David Leavitt should be regarded as a seer. Sarah Dunant seemed to find something unique in David Leavitt as a creator of 'gay life in the suburbs.' What kind of worlds does she think the rest of us inhabit? Pink ghettoes on remote Scottish islands, I imagine, where we compose novels merely for and about each other, so that the general reading public in Britain can safely go on pretending we don't exist. *The Late Show* needs to have a good look at itself: ostensibly an arts programme, it – and its presenters – appear to feel more at ease with ephemera such as pop and fashion. It's becoming a televisual *Time Out*.

An interesting postscript to this episode was added by Peter Parker in *The Sunday Correspondent*. In a piece called *Coming Out With Panache*, written to acknowledge the tenth anniversary of the founding of Gay Men's Press, Parker quotes Ben Goldstein, GMP's new and very young fiction editor (twenty-three), who complains of 'a dearth of good gay fiction in England, and is looking to America, which he thinks most English homosexuals see as the home of "the real gay experience." ' Let me, thirty years his senior in experience, tell Mr Goldstein that neither I, nor any other British gay man I've ever met, thinks gay life in the United States more 'real' than cruising the bars or falling in love in Birmingham, Edinburgh, Bristol or Brighton, though we've all certainly enjoyed our hols in San Francisco and New York. What does he mean, anyway, by 'real'? Perhaps good British gay fiction is being sent to other desks than his, and if this leads to GMP flooding the market with American imports I, for one, will not be reading them. There are already available here, courtesy of Alyson Publications, quite enough high-school romances – their Salingerese protagonists sounding as if they'd come straight out of the pages of *The Catcher in the Rye* – and torrid passions between the locker-room jockstraps.

BYZANTINE – THREE

> … I have sailed the seas and come
> To the holy city of Byzantium.

But the truth is I've flown on a Turkish Airlines jet to Istanbul. Where are Phidias' ivories, the golden grasshoppers and bees, the unpurged images of day, Hades' bobbin bound in mummy-cloth, that dolphin-torn and gong-tormented sea? Only in Yeats's poems: artefacts of eternity. The city built on the ruins of Constantine's is strangely like Stoke Newington – twentieth-century, drab and shabby, car-polluted, full of noisy Turks dropping endless amounts of litter onto the pavements. The Emperor's pavements where an agony of flame cannot singe a sleeve!

Surely Santa Sophia will put me in touch with Constantinople. It does! Despite the loss of most of its splendours in 1204 and 1453, it is a miracle of rare device, more vast and magnificent than I could ever imagine. Taking only five years to build, its technology was a thousand years ahead of its time. Justinian, in 532, ordered that it should be 'like nothing seen before since the day of Adam or can be seen in the future,' and so it is. Here are the mosaic emperors and empresses; Leo the Sixth kneeling before Christ, John the Second, Irene, Zoe, Constantine the Great himself. Holding their bags of dust. From the Emperors' door in the narthex to the huge, whispering space of the cathedral proper: absorbing the complexities of its shadows, its ghosts. Being dazzled by the light streaming through its glass; being overwhelmed by the size of its seemingly unsupported and floating dome; being dwarfed, rendered insignificant, but still a receptor

147

of a mass of pleasurable sensations – a dome that disdains all that man is, the fury and the mire of human veins… What other resonances? A bas-relief of dolphins, those guides to the underworld; and the round pendants that hang from the main columns – nineteenth-century additions when Santa Sophia was a mosque – recall the great cathedral gong that was struck at curfew.

But the mosaics in the Kariye monastery are the finest. Much less formal and stiff than those in Santa Sophia or St Mark's, Venice, they achieve what I'd have thought the medium itself would have made impossible – they flow, they swirl, they tell stories as paintings do, are light and graceful, convey an amazing sense of movement. Two of the bewildered dead are being pulled with the speed of a rocket out of their sepulchres by a dancing Christ; weird, wrapped, sleeping figures are like Henry Moore sculptures or foetuses in wombs; dogs bark; horses take fright; wine is spilled; people fly through the air: and they were made almost seven hundred years before the birth of Chagall. Close by are the city walls, built by Theodosius the Second fourteen hundred years ago and still impressive bastions, though pierced now by motorways and other twentieth-century horrors. I climb to the top of them, worried by the dizzying height and unrailed sheer drop, and spoil my pleasure in the views by near-panic about how to get down without breaking my neck. No envious barbarian – Goth, Magyar, Bulgar, Slav, Frank, Serb or Turk – conquered them until 1453 when Mehmet the Second arrived with his cannon.

The monuments in the Hippodrome, where sixty thousand people once watched charioteers, time and the weather have battered beyond interest, but the tree-lined open space is pleasant in this crowded city. The trees are planes, flourishing as they do in London, on smog. It is only mid-September, but leaves are brown already and falling. Autumn comes early here and stays long. A pleasing mock-Byzantine fountain stands at the north end of the Hippodrome, a gift to Sultan Abdul Hamid the Second from – of all people – Kaiser Wilhelm the Second. Not far away are the underground cisterns Justinian built. I imagine a cold, dank encounter, but the air is warm and fresh, and wooden walkways solve the problem of drowned feet. Another moment of excitement: an immense forest of pillars and arches, with carved acanthus-leaf capitals, extending in all directions. It is like entering the mosque at Córdova. Submerged floodlights illuminate the columns, the domes. A cathédrale engloutie. But I could do without the peculiar psychedelic music that is coming from invisible loudspeakers: Mantovani heard from the bottom of a bath.

And that is all of any significance. The fate of the Queen of Cities was sealed, I suppose, in 1204, and 1453 finished her off. The subsequent five centuries of Islam have not helped. The totally opposite emotions produced by the two extreme ends of southern Europe – Rumelian Turkey and Andalusian Spain – keep coming into my mind. In Granada and Córdova one constantly regrets the destruction of Islamic civilization, the dull palaces and cathedrals Charles the Fifth erected in what were exquisite masterpieces of Arab architecture. The expulsion of the Moors seems a terrible crime, the Reconquest a fearful mistake, Isabella and Ferdinand barbarians compared with those who lost the battles. In Istanbul it is the other way round: if only Constantine the Eleventh had been able to afford Urban's cannon! If Urban had only sold his armoury to anyone other than Mehmet! For the Ottomans behaved as Charles the Fifth behaved. The mosaics were whitewashed, the treasures smashed. And like Christian Spain, Ottoman Turkey produced nothing to equal what was destroyed. The décor of the Blue Mosque and the Mosque of Süleyman the Magnificent hold one's attention, but architecturally they are pale imitations of Santa Sophia. (The Small Sophia, though, is a delight – simple, peaceful, musty – and that is because it was not built by the Ottomans; it is a fifth-century Byzantine church which, a thousand years later, had its interior Islamicised.) Istanbul's mosques are a repetitive experience; large or small, there is little variety in their design. Every minaret in this city of a thousand minarets is almost exactly alike. Seen one, seen the lot.

Topkapi compared with Granada's Alhambra is of no importance. Its fabric second-rate, its gardens and court-yards dull, its fountains uninteresting, this palace is only remarkable for the huge quantity of expensive objects it contains – cart-loads of jewels, swords, daggers, helmets, costumes, gold, silver, porcelain, china, ceramics, minia-tures, and the glittering junk the crowned heads of Europe gave to the sultans. I'm glad, however, to see the Topkapi diamond – simply because I enjoyed the film – and the views from the innermost courtyard are superb. In front of me is the Golden Horn, still as busy with ships as it was in the eras of any of the Constantines, beyond it the Genoese quarter, Galata, with its famous tower; to my right the Bosphorus and Leander's Tower, behind me the Sea of Marmara. The most endearing aspect of this city is that one is always aware of water: not as much as in Venice, but there are similar moments of stone, sea and light dancing in harmony. Water makes the climate very agreeable – it is rarely too hot – and the Russian winds that can sweep over the Black Sea and chill the northern end of the Bosphorus on the sunniest summer days have become, by the time they've arrived here, gentle, warm breezes.

There is much to dislike about Istanbul, however. You cannot leave your hotel at any hour without being accosted by street traders, many of them mere children, trying to sell you postcards, cassettes, films for the cam-era, leather belts, even pairs of socks. It occurs all over the city; they pester and persist. One knows it will happen in the bazaar, but the aggressiveness of bazaar salesmen is annoying. They approach you, speaking in English: the conversation almost always follows the same pattern –

'Hullo.'

'Hullo.'

'Are you interested in buying leather goods?' (or car-pets, tiles, pottery, hookahs, whatever.)

'No.'

Very loudly and unpleasantly: '*Why not?*'

Turks can be charming and helpful; they will go out of their way to put you in the right direction or solve a language problem, or to make sure you catch the correct bus – but where money is concerned too many of them cheat, lie and rob. A favourite trick is a rapid sleight-of-hand with the twenty thousand lire note (about six pounds); 'You gave me one thousand!' they yell, brandishing the note of that denomination in your face. It happened to me with a taxi-driver, and I saw a German tourist on a boat being similarly bamboozled. A dishonest clerk at the bus station charged me double the going rate to Canakkale, and I didn't realise it until I was crossing the Dardanelles. And when buying anything from a street trader, or food from the urchins who throng the buses when they stop, the exact money is essential; when you discover you've been short-changed these little thieves have disappeared.

One could be forgiven for thinking the whole of Turkey is now one vast building site. Nineteenth-century houses are few, even in central Istanbul. There are some unbelievably dreary post-war suburbs that stretch on and on for miles; they look like the worst areas of outer Prague, Madrid, London, Detroit, anywhere. For about a hundred miles west of Istanbul, the north shore of the Sea of Marmara resembles any Costa del Crap, covered with standard internat-flat-block-grot. The coast here is not particularly interesting, nor is the hinterland of the plain of Thrace, but that doesn't excuse. The builders who erect this concrete litter ought to be shot. And along the concrete ribbons that link these hideous monsters of towns, the traffic noses forward like giant sightless fish from some ocean depth, groping its way through a sea of smog. Where is the inexplicable splendour of Ionian white and gold?

Turkey wants to become a member of the E.E.C. and is rather annoyed that its application to join has not, a year on, been answered. Its record on human rights issues, however, comes nowhere near to fulfilling some of the basic requirements of the Treaty of Rome: the English-language daily paper, which I was reading one morning at breakfast, said there were two hundred and forty-four prisoners in jail at the moment awaiting execution for a variety of different offences. Also the country's hygiene is well below the minimum standards the Common Market would demand. Nobody I know has returned from a holiday in Turkey without diarrhoea: the state of the drinking water is the problem – 'Don't even clean your teeth in it,' my doctor said. According to the paper I was reading, rumours about an outbreak of cholera in the south-eastern region of the country were false, but it was possible that there were cases of dysentery and typhoid. Despite all the precautions I took, I soon found I had a virulent stomach bug, and threadworms – the latter, I guess, from contaminated meat in a shish kebab.

But it is the Islamic nature of present Turkish society that I find most discomforting. Atatürk wanted to construct a secular, socialist, Western society, and while he and his henchman, Inönü, were alive, Turkey was reluctantly dragged out of the Middle Ages. Since 1950, however, with political power largely in the hands of the traditionalist right, it has regressed, even though three military coups have attempted to restore Atatürk's aims and values. Women appear to be rare creatures in Istanbul. Very occasionally one sees them, always in headscarves, lugging bags of groceries and shepherding children; and in middle-class institutions such as banks they work behind the counters, here minus the head covering. All the traders are men; no woman drives a car, and if a woman is eating in a restaurant or drinking in a café she is almost certainly a foreign tourist. Though women clean the rooms, hotels are run by men – does this explain the absence of toilet paper in most of the loos? The Bosphorus has an abundance of fish, but it is very hard to find a restaurant that serves fish. Real Men, I suppose, Eat Meat. Turkish men en masse, with their identikit dark trousers, white shirts, and regulation black moustaches, seem childish to me – honking their car horns and driving like maniacs, passing their leisure hours exclusively with other men in cafés, cheering the football game on TV. Monotonous, like the minarets.

Only once do I have a glimpse of a society more like our

own. On my way to the mosque of Süleyman the Magnificent, I decide to take a short cut through the grounds of the University. It is, I imagine, the interval between lectures – the courtyards are full of students discussing, laughing, reading books, looking at the notes they have made. There are as many women as men; no head coverings or skirts that reach the ground. Women alone, in pairs, in groups, in groups with men, holding hands with or kissing their boyfriends. Just like my students at Exeter or California State, San José: I feel benevolent and professorial. But I am in for a rude shock when I try to leave the campus. The only way out is the way I have come in. There is Süleyman's mosque, a stone's throw distant, but between it and me is a very high wall surmounted by iron railings, impossible to climb. It encircles the whole campus: a dangerous hazard if the students all rush, in the event of a fire or a bomb explosion, to leave at once. It is as if Islam has said that a university is a necessary evil – a hotbed of liberal attitudes and Western ideas, best kept safely behind bars.

A trip by boat from the Golden Horn up the Bosphorus, as far as the Black Sea: a day of all weathers – heat, sun, cloud, wind, rain. Steep hills, in parts almost like cliffs, rise up on both sides of the water, and on these hills are the sultans' summer palaces, the villas of the middle classes and the rich, the mansions of nineteenth-century ambassadors and government ministers. The Dardanelles is gentler, less populated, somehow more ancient, but the Bosphorus is clear and a sparkling blue; in places a subtle, deep turquoise. There is much to see as we head north – Florence Nightingale's hospital at Scutari; Leander's Tower (misnamed, for it was the Hellespont – the Dardanelles – across which he swam): the present structure is eighteenth-century, but it has been a lighthouse since the first Constantine; Rumelia Hisari, Mehmet the Second's superb fort; the two modern suspension bridges that link Europe and Asia like giant steel pins and carry the motorway that now surrounds Istanbul more effectively than the walls of Theodosius; decayed but still splendid waterfront palazzi, reminiscent of Venice in their architectural styles, decoration, and their rotting steps and crumbling basements; the ships – this is a crowded, international shipping lane – some flying Russian, Czech or Rumanian flags; the seashore villages which look more attractive the further they are from Istanbul. Finally, a tantalising glimpse of the Black Sea, and it does look black and a little sinister compared with the friendly blue of the Bosphorus, but that is maybe because of the dark mist on the horizon, beyond which is Russia: a cold, Siberian wind is blowing from Yalta, bringing rain. Out there, between us and the mist, is an enormous flock of birds flying west-wards. Round the corner is Bulgaria; to the east, Trebizond and the relics of other fabulous toy empires.

The boat turns and chugs south, docking at Anadolu Kavaği on the Asian side. A picture-postcard village, old houses huddled under plane trees some of which are larger and more ancient than any I've seen in London. Platanus: great survivor. The waterfront urchins shout their wares – tiles, plates, the menus in nearby restaurants, yet more leather belts and socks. Fish, hauled out of the Bosphorus an hour ago, are grilled on charcoal fires at the quay's edge. The smell is delicious, and I'm sorry I opted for sandwiches on the boat. I have not set foot in Asia for twenty-seven years – a warmer Asia; Lebanon, Jordan, Israel. The chill Russian rain begins to fall in earnest.

I stare across the water to the Europe I've just left and say to myself, look! I have made an exit. And so I have – I've left behind the world of novels, short stories, poems, children's books and critical essays, and I'm staring across the divide between them and this: my first real travel piece.

HOW IT IS

For me, the problems the virus has caused so far are very low levels of energy, isolation, and distress – the latter as much the result of many gay men's responses to HIV as the responses of straight people or the hysterical lies concocted by the tabloid press.

There are days – not many, fortunately – when I am so tired that I'm asleep before lunchtime; mostly I hold out until early afternoon. Mornings are good: I can think, I can concentrate, I deal with Third House business; I read, I can – once in a while – write a little. Though there is almost nothing to write about now. I feel disjoined from the rest of the human race. Afternoons, when I've slept, I potter, or just stare out of the open French windows at my garden, which is beautiful this long, heat-wave summer. Evenings I sleep again, watch hours of mindless television, and force myself to cook. I'm not fit enough to do anything else. Days pass when I see no one, speak to no one except the woman next door, assistants in shops, friends on the phone. I have no lover. I'm the sole inhabitant of this big old house, and I rattle around in it, a small pea in a large pod, and I don't now want that to change. I couldn't cope with a lover. I couldn't cope with a lodger. In theory my younger son, Adam, lives here too, but he's abroad in tent city somewhere; I haven't seen him since 1988. The winter winds may drive him home like a migrating bird: I'm not even sure I could cope with *that*.

I put it at its most woebegone. I'd be the first to admit that the virus, though the prime cause of lassitude, is not the sole cause. There's a strong psychological element; and, just as energy creates energy, so lack of energy

155

begets a greater lack. There have been whole days this summer when I've weeded my garden, planted flowers, and not had to rest; friends have been to stay – I've enjoyed their company and showing them Torquay and Sidmouth and the still enchanted wartime home of my childhood, Welcombe, on the North Devon cliffs. I can enjoy a dinner party. I can't now manage an evening in the pub too often, despite the anticipated pleasure of acquaintances, gossip, and staring at attractive men; but I've sometimes done so. One night I even danced for a quarter of an hour. And I've had sex: four times in eight months! Wow! No use thinking of the times, not so long ago, when I was having sex every day of the week. I do think about it, of course. But the most recent man – a casual pick-up; I don't even know his name – was superbly good-looking and enthusiastic. Despite all the necessary safety precautions, I thoroughly enjoyed myself.

Tiredness isn't the only problem. Oral thrush and gingivitis are an unpleasant combination, but usually controllable with antibiotics, and my antigen level – the marker of viral activity – is still high, though interferon has brought it down a little. Injecting myself three times a week is a nuisance. No more than a nuisance – four months' practice means I can do it without hurting myself. Even so, a certain amount of will-power is required to stick a needle in one's leg. I've just started on the maximum dosage, which will probably blow my head off, or at least cause nausea, migraine, and blocked sinuses. If this doesn't lower the antigen level considerably in the next two months, the doctor in charge of the experiment will conclude that, though it may work with some HIV patients, interferon doesn't work for me. AZT is the only alternative. I've decided I will not take AZT unless – until – I develop full-blown AIDS. It's too toxic. The thought of anaemia and frequent blood transfusions, and the likely diminution of an already poor quality of existence, means AZT, as far as I'm concerned, is a drastic last resort.

The deterioration of the skin has led to my developing, for only the second time in my life, an allergy. To a plant in the garden – it sounds absurd – called comfrey, the leaves of which, even more absurdly, have healing properties; they are said to cure bruises. Touching this rampant, hairy object gives me ulcers and soreness as nasty as excessive sunburn. I could destroy it, but my ex-wife planted it years ago and, though she doesn't live in this house, she's still fond of the thing. It grows like mad and the flowers nearby – montbretia, astilbe, scabious, London pride – take umbrage; so I moved it recently to an obscure corner where I don't need to touch it or chop it about. But despite precautions it brushed against my skin. Result: two swollen, blistered, painful arms.

The virus has produced a chronic dermatitis on my face – the skin is as red as if I lived perpetually in Qatar, and scaly: sometimes puffy. I began to develop a severe ache in both eyes I was sure was not the consequence of too much close work or the need for stronger reading glasses. The opinion of the doctor at the local eye hospital was that the dermatitis had got onto the corneas and dried up all the fluids; it was – and is – easily, painlessly curable by squirting artificial tears into the eyes. He said, however, that there were signs of premature ageing, and, he went on, he knew nothing about the damage HIV might have directly caused, nothing about cytomegalovirus. Panic! Relieved fairly soon afterwards by a thorough examination in London. No AIDS damage, no cytomegalovirus, nothing inconsistent with what the eyes of a man in his fifties should be, except for the dry corneas: just squirt drops in, as and when I feel it necessary.

Prince Andrew Bolkonsky in *War and Peace* says to himself as he is dying, 'The living cannot understand that all these feelings that are so dear to them – all these thoughts which seem so important, really do not matter. No, we have ceased to meet on common ground.' Though not near death, I can see what he means; I feel that too. Most obviously in a gay bar as I watch men pursuing a pretty face or recently bereaved men frantically looking for substitutes, as I listen to tales of conquest or what X is like in the sack or the idle chitchat and tittle-tattle of any crowd speculating on some newcomer. I am cut off from this – there *is* no common ground now. It seems so futile. I am, therefore, cut off from the constituency that gave me so much material to write about: all the novels and short stories from *The Milkman's On His Way* to *Quince* and *The Colour of His Hair*. And the usual, everyday pleasures and problems of others – work, home improvements, what 'we' did, what 'we' said, 'our' holiday plans, 'our' difficulties with parents or bosses or lovers. They're less important to me: as if I were reading about them in a book.

Prince Andrew's remark, if put the other way round, is also true. Very few people have any understanding, or wish to understand, what *I* am thinking and feeling. This is real isolation. Almost no one, not even thoroughly experienced glad-to-be-gay men, has any desire to stare AIDS in the face, come to terms with it, learn to regard it as just another life-threatening illness; it is – particularly in provincial gay communities – the ultimate unmentionable: 'We don't want to know.' A friend said to me last week that he thought I was very brave to be so open, that he admired my honesty. I don't feel I'm being brave: I simply cannot lie about it. Or hush it up. That would be too contrary to my nature, to my whole moral self. And I was aware, when we were talking, that he found my openness frightening and uncomfortable, that he saw my role in our gay world as a disturbing and perhaps distasteful Cassandra.

Closer friends than he is – gay and straight – and members of my family are no help, either; they will not act, as I've said earlier in this book, as dead-letterboxes in which I can post my dark thoughts. They need to reassure, to argue, to refute – it's perfectly understandable – because what I have to say also frightens them, makes them think of their own mortality, embarrasses the even tenor of their lives. How much nicer, I'm sure they say to themselves, if only I'd just shut up! Then they could praise my rectitude, that decent British reserve – so much commented on in obituaries – which keeps the sick and the dying silent about their symptoms, their fears, their suffering, their isolation from others. It is indeed *not* to be praised, but deplored: the proper response, in my view, to a life-threatening disease which cuts men down in their prime is not to go gentle, but to rage, rage against the dying of the light ... All those eulogies about reserve and silence are merely expressions of relief that sick men don't embarrass us; we are able to move on, ungripped by the Ancient Mariner's skinny hand.

The gay community often congratulates itself on how well it deals with AIDS, particularly in its practice of safe sex, fund-raising for charities, the love and devotion it has shown to the sick and the dying. And so it should, for it's true – up to a point. The only comment I've seen about how badly many – yes, many – gay men behave was in *The Pink Paper*, in an article by Steve Anders (Issue 79) and in a letter from 'Michael' (Issue 81.) Steve Anders, who has ARC, says that when he was ill his gay friends, gay neighbours and ex-lovers didn't even visit him, let alone offer to help; he was 'the bad news of the block.' In support groups, he says, he hears 'the same story over and over again,' and he quotes some examples – a twenty-year-old with AIDS who discussed his problems on television and as a result was 'beaten up outside the Copacabana by other gay men;' a lesbian with ARC 'spat upon and thrown out of a women's bar;' a man, blinded by AIDS, 'not allowed to call a taxi in the manager's office of the Coleherne.' Michael wrote in to say that he 'recently picked up a very dishy twenty-one-year-old' who took him home for sex; this youth wanted to be fucked without a condom because Michael 'looked well and didn't look gay.' 'With my cock standing to attention,' Michael continues, 'and him with his legs spread and high in the air, I told him that I had ARC and that my boyfriend had died a few months ago.' The young man then threw him out; 'I walked home,' Michael says, 'with aching balls, not being able to make sense of the situation.'

One must treat these stories cautiously, but ... 'didn't look gay!' Those silly adverts in the personal columns: 'Must be twenty-two to twenty-eight and straight-looking, straight-acting.' The straightjackets we invent for ourselves! How appallingly ageist we are! Two decades after Stonewall how self-oppressive! What's wrong with being twenty-one and a clone, or a wee bit camp? Is the desired object less lovable because he has a moustache, or flaps the occasional wrist, is twenty-one, or thirty-five ('a very good age,' Lady Bracknell said), or forty-six or fifty-three, or older?

I too have met men in the years since I've been diagnosed HIV positive who wanted unsafe sex with me; I can well understand how difficult it must have been for Michael, cock three miles high and a delicious youth with legs half-way up to the ceiling, to resist temptation and explain. I know no examples, personally, of HIV or AIDS sufferers (yes, I will call us sufferers and victims, for that is how I see myself, and I can think of no reason to change normal linguistic usage because some pressure group says I should) who have been beaten up or thrown out of bars; but I do have my own examples of bad behaviour that sicken and anger me. Those idiotic young queens who think AIDS is confined to clones, or to sexually passive men who only want to get fucked, or to us older gays who are now being punished – justly, they will even say – for our nineteen-seventies sleeping around. When I learned that I was HIV positive, my lover at that time considered it to be a reward I deserved for adventures in San Francisco; despite the fact that, as I had a lover in that city, my adventures there were minimal. (And my account of them in *A Better Class of Blond* largely fictitious.) He – I don't mean the California lover – was diagnosed HIV positive at about the same time as I was, and blamed me: I was no longer a marvellous person, charismatic, beautiful, great in bed – but merely a bag of deadly viruses, which, if he stayed with me, would quickly put him beneath his tombstone. He wouldn't let me fuck him even with a condom, wouldn't suck my cock, but it was all right, he thought, for me to suck *his* cock, for him to fuck me, with or without a condom. I suppose it was a refusal to admit to himself that he really was carrying the virus. He soon departed, for a previous lover who hadn't had a test; it was 'safer', he said. Not – clearly – for the previous lover, but that didn't seem to concern him any more than the possibility that his viruses might have come from somebody else, years ago; that *he* might have infected *me*.

160

The question of blame is irrelevant and absurd; like crossing the road, sex is always a risk of sorts. Crossing the road is a decision for which the responsibility is one's own, and so is sleeping with another man. The refusal to admit responsibility, the lies people tell, the deceptions they practise: the number of times we are told a person died of cancer or some other disease when in truth it was AIDS-related; an acquaintance of mine who will not admit that his lover, who died some years ago, had AIDS, because he can't bear to think that he might be HIV positive himself; the doctor who wanted to attend the funeral of one of his AIDS patients, but didn't because the cause of the death was hushed up – he felt his presence might raise embarrassing questions about why he was there. I would have assumed he was just another friend. And what is so wrong with announcing that one has AIDS, that somebody one knows has died of it? Every man's death diminishes me, and so do every man's lies. Each lie about AIDS pushes us – HIV and AIDS sufferers in particular – back a step.

Of course one has to take cognizance of wishes for privacy; and blurting out information from the roof-tops that would lead to a man being dismissed from his employment, or being told to quit by his landlord, or attracting the muckraking of the tabloid press, would be immoral and utterly reprehensible. (The press, it seems to me, is rarely interested in those who are honest: in their witch-hunts they don't usually persecute out, glad-to-be-gay men, though there are exceptions.) A few years back, some people I know (who, coincidentally, happen to work for the local AIDSline) were much offended by a piece I wrote for *Man Alive* about private AIDS testing; in it I mentioned the behaviour of the ex-lover I've just discussed, and of another ex-lover who, knowing he was HIV positive, formed a relationship with a man – they are still together – and did not reveal he was carrying the virus. I used false names, but the offended people considered that some mutual friends and acquaintances would know who I was talking about. I had committed a gross breach of confidentiality; I was to be ignored, shunned. A bit childish – were they so afraid of me they couldn't tell me what they thought? I've breached confidentiality no more than Michael, in his letter to *The Pink Paper*, has breached it; yes, he and I have both spoken of men whose identity a handful of others might work out, but much more important in my opinion is the need to say that ruthless, selfish dishonesty still exists, that it isn't everyone who has responded marvellously to the AIDS crisis, and, because there are plenty of shits around, there must be no let-up in safer sex practices.

There is a man in our local community who, others are convinced, has AIDS, and indeed some of his problems are compatible with AIDS-related symptoms; but I see no reason to doubt what we have been told by his lover. Perhaps I'm being naive. But the suspicion, prurience, fear, and deception accompanying AIDS mean that we have only to cough in a gay bar and everyone thinks we have pneumocystis carinii. It has become difficult to say that we've lost weight, or have diarrhoea, or that we sweat at night – the latter not exactly a unique event this long, hot summer. The history of AIDS has been remarkably similar to the histories of other epidemics in the past, accounts of which we find in Defoe's *Journal of the Plague Year*, Thomas Shapter's *The Cholera in Exeter*, novels like Camus's *La Peste*, films like Bergman's *Seventh Seal*. They record what we, too, witness: pain and suffering, love, devotion, bravery, heroism; and also sheer folly, almost unbelievable selfishness, and downright wickedness. And myths – the doctors have got it wrong, we're all going to die, there's no harm in carrying on just as we were, if we change our diet we'll be cured, it happens to other people, it happens in other countries, it's the scourge of God, avoid doorknobs. Human nature doesn't change.

I don't think it's brought out the best in me, or the worst. Yet. I suppose I could act, when I do have the energy, to alleviate some of the isolation I feel; I can be criticised for allowing the virus to make me too introspective; I may well be accused of too much pessimism – though I see my own cast of mind as stoic rather than pessimistic. I've done little to help others: I could have given time to Body Positive when I lived in London, raised cash for Lighthouse, and so on. I don't, however, see my strengths as being along those lines; gregarious I am, but I'm not a joiner. What I do best is with words, paper, pen, and I'm more than willing to use that in the cause of understanding and demythologising AIDS, though I imagine this essay will arouse hostility rather than welcome in some sections of the community.

I can't help that. It's how it is.

TROY

A long journey; it reminded me of Eliot's *Magi*, 'A cold coming we had of it ... ' But it wasn't cold, merely uncomfortable on a crowded, smoky bus through a land of sunflowers and cement-coloured earth. And the villages, though dirty, weren't charging high prices; nor did voices sing in our ears that this was all folly. Through Gallipoli, Gelibolu in Turkish – woods and water – and over the Dardanelles on a creaking, ancient ferry. Canakkale, late September late afternoon. It was (you may say) satisfactory. Next morning another bus, through scented pine-woods fledging the wild-ridged mountains, the sea below to our right, the deepest blue imaginable. An old white horse ...

Troy.

I stand on the ramparts and gaze across flat, fertile fields – peasants bent double; cotton, sunflowers, vegetables of all kinds – to the sea, to the point where the Hellespont joins the Aegean, and wait for the arrival of ships. Hector, Paris, even Helen, may have stood on this exact spot, waiting. Have the Greeks already disembarked, are now out of sight behind the low hills to the south? Menelaus in a bad temper. Agamemnon, unaware of the awful fate Clytemnestra is preparing for him. Achilles in his tent with Patroclus, making ecstatic love.

The fields were probably just as fertile then, though the crops may have been different. It explains why Troy is here: enough to feed a whole city. And close to the sea, a good place to keep an eye on who may be slipping in and out of the Hellespont.

The site is not vast like Ephesus: I'm glad; I can assimilate it. Know my bearings. I'm glad, too, that it's so far off the beaten track – not spoiled by tramping hordes of tourists. There are some, Germans mostly, in conducted parties having everything explained. There's no need to have anything explained! And I'm also glad Troy is excavated only in part. It isn't a museum, elaborately ticketed for our inspection: the mind, the memory, the imagination are allowed to be charged with an extraordinary flare. To be set free.

In a narrow street between walls two and a half thousand years old, I hear them: the shouts, the cries, the thumps, the clash of swords on shields. For about twenty seconds; as soon as I realise what is happening the noise is gone. Oh, sure, projection of course; I'm simply giving flesh to the ghosts in my mind. But I actually *heard* it – it was outside of me. Others, I've been told, have had the same experience. Did I see them too? If I did, it was the faintest hint of tunics, helmets, swords. Paris ... yes: blond hair. And blond hair on his muscly legs.

Or is it a memory of Bamber Gascoigne as Paris in a Marlowe Society production of Shakespeare's *Troilus and Cressida*, thirty-three years ago when he and I were both undergraduates at Cambridge? I slept in his bed one night. Not like Helen; he wasn't in it with me.

But I *saw* him.

I look again for ships, Triton blowing his wreathed horn. On the far side of the Dardanelles is the huge memorial to the thousands who died there so needlessly in 1915. Two and a half millenia separate these gigantic battles; their causes were of equal stupidity. Their geographical closeness astonishes me. The astonishing stillness of the dead.

> Civilization is hooped together, brought
> Under a rule, under the semblance of peace
> By manifold illusion; but man's life is thought,
> And he, despite his terror, cannot cease
> Ravening through century after century,
> Ravening, raging, and uprooting that he may come
> Into the desolation of reality:
> Egypt and Greece, good-bye, and good-bye, Rome!

This is a holy place, an encantada: I have never been

anywhere so vibrant with significance. Though if I knew nothing of history, if I had not read Homer's *Iliad* and loved it, would it just be a pile of battered stones?

I feel whole and sane, at peace with all things.

Good-bye!

Third House (Publishers)
New Books 1989

TOUCHING HARRY   Peter Robins
A book about the tragedy and the comedy of growing up
gay in the closing years of World War Two.
    "A novel of acute insight into the sometimes painful rites
of passage from adolescence to adulthood" — *Capital Gay*
        ISBN 1 870188 09 8

THE COLOUR OF HIS HAIR   David Rees
A novel about two gay teenagers whose relationship leads
to persecution at school and a surprising denouement ten
years later.
    "Poised, delicate and full of insight ... Rees writing at his
best" — *The Pink Paper*
        ISBN 1 870188 10 1

**THE FREEZER COUNTER   edited by David Rees and
Peter Robins**
A collection of nineteen stories including contributions
from Tom Wakefield, Patrick Gale, Michael Carson, Peter
Burton, Gregory Woods, David Rees and Peter Robins.
    "An intriguing collection of all too rare new writing ... an
essential anthology" — *City Limits*
        ISBN 1 870188 11 X

New Books 1990
PLEASING THE PUNTERS   Dave Royle
A first book by a gifted young writer. This collection of
stories is full of compassionate and humorous observation
of people trying to make sense of the world.
ISBN 1 870188 13 6   To be published May 1990

STONY GLANCES   Peter Robins
A fifth collection of new stories by this well-established
writer whose work has a controlled elegance that makes it a
delight to read.
ISBN 1 870188 14 4   To be published September 1990

WEEKEND   Martin Foreman
A novel of deep emotions set against erotic attraction. With
his relationship in crisis, the central character remembers
earlier lovers and tries to understand what went wrong.
ISBN 1 870188 15 2   To be published November 1990